P9-EEM-036

THE WINTER

OF THE

FISHER

THE WINTER OF THE FISHER

Cameron Langford

W · W · NORTON & COMPANY · INC · NEW YORK

Printed in the United States of America

Library of Congress Catalog Card No. 77-139382

SBN 393 08638 0

2 3 4 5 6 7 8 9 0

To

Margaret Langford

for her faith

THE WINTER OF THE FISHER

The setting sun will always
set me to rights—or if a
sparrow come before my window,
I take part in its existence
and pick about the gravel.

—Keats to Bailey

PROLOGUE

His first awareness was of being born, of shifting pressures and liquid movement, of cold that set his blood racing, and of the startling sensation as his lungs expanded with musky, heavy air. Then the newborn world crashed in on him in such a jumble of touch and taste and smell, of softness and warmth and sound, that he could only huddle mewling under the onslaught. He remembered the awful shock of birth for possibly forty-eight hours, and then the images faded and were gone, buried so deeply in the recesses of his infant brain that he would never call them forth again. And that was as it should be, for the memory was of no use to him. Besides, by then he had discovered taste.

For the next two weeks, the world was his mother's nipple. He clung to it whenever she was near, searched for it when she was not, and scrambled feverishly over the others to find it the moment he sensed she had returned. At the fortnight's end he began to understand about the others, that the soft, squirming forms he pushed away in his search for milk were not mere obstacles, but individual, living creatures that squalled and squirmed and sucked, and even smelled the same as he. Together, they numbered four, and that was good; four was the extent of their mother's milk supply.

His next piece of knowledge was that the world, this strange, blind limbo of food, warmth, and security, was not a changeless world. The texture of the air varied, as did the temperature. Smells came and went, and sounds. There was a dim, red light beyond his tightly sealed eyelids, and later only blackness. His mother vanished and then returned, and there seemed to be no order to it all until, after a week, he began to sort out his first pattern. Coolness came with the dark, and his mother left. Warmth was married to the light and his mother's return. On days when her fur was dry, she lay against the back wall of the den. Wetness took her to the other side, and she pressed against the entrance to keep any further wet from trickling in.

By the fourth week, he had discovered the usefulness of movement. He learned to heave himself to his feet and instead of crawling, waddled. He blundered around the dark den whenever his mother was not there, tripping and staggering and bumping into the walls, and once even tottering half out the entrance before the night sounds drove him trembling back. With movement came the revelation that different objects had different smells, and he spent excited hours trying to give meaning to them all. He learned the milky, fecal scent of his litter mates, the sun-drenched fragrance of old, dried grass, the rich musk of fur, the pungent, fruity aroma of earth, and the sap-sweet scent of spruce roots. But three long weeks were to pass before he could give the smells a shape.

One morning in the seventh week, he awoke to a

crack of blazing light, pouring in through eyelids shuttered since birth. The shattering brilliance stabbed along his nerves and into his brain. It was his first experience with pain. Howling miserably, he scrabbled in a rickety circle and tried to put his paw across his snout. Finally, he escaped by burying his head beneath his mother's flank. Almost immediately she rose and slipped outside the den, leaving him squalling half in fear and half from anger. He stopped only when she returned to block off the light by plugging the entrance with dead grass and last year's leaves.

Another week; his eyes were fully opened, and he had learned to control them well enough to see his mother clearly. Her size startled him. One day, entering the den, she frightened him from the warm depths of dreaming, and he snarled his first infant challenge. Then he caught the wonderfully familiar milk, musk and mother smell, and tottered forward hungrily. She was mother, and she was food, and so he loved her deeply.

He was too young, too animal to understand how incredibly beautiful she was. Her lithe body was slightly under three feet long, and though she was large for a female fisher, her son would eventually top her by a foot. More than a third of her length was tail, but even its magnificence was surpassed by the depth and luster of her coat. Honeyed highlights danced deep in the rich brown under-fiber through which longer, darker guard hairs grew, adding a brilliant, changing texture to the subtly shifting tones. Her head was a triangle from which glowed two exceptionally intelligent eyes, their calm wisdom enhanced by the faint silver grizzling of the guard hairs across her head and shoulders. Her fangs, when they were revealed, were obviously those of an animal that knew precisely how to care for herself and her kittens. Or perhaps the impression of enormous competence was in her body and the way she moved. She was strikingly slender. Not thin, but slender, with the sculptured sleekness that reveals an inward, controlled power and strength. When she moved, it was like willows weeping in the wind.

The young fisher stayed in the den beneath the old spruce for five more long weeks, and during that time was visited by his first great tragedy. His mother's milk dried up. The first time she came to him with empty udders, he pummeled and sucked and nibbled so hard, she cuffed him across the den. When he set up a high, wavering wail of indignation, she cuffed him again. Late that evening, she returned and dropped a rusty-colored, furry bundle before her four kittens. They turned up there noses and quavered pitifully for milk. The mother fisher stalked away, muttering. Finally the young fisher was driven to dab his tongue at the dark red smear on the dead mouse's skull. The hunger for milk died as he bit down, for he know that this was the taste he had been born for, the salty, satisfying tang of blood.

And now the world beyond became a fascination. Time and time again, and more with every passing day, he would slip away from his sleeping mother and, leading his sister and two brothers, scamper outside on the shelving rocks to blink in the glorious sunshine, sniff the incredible variety of shifting July smells, and lose himself in rollicking tussling matches with his fellows. But never for too long. Five minutes, possibly ten, and his mother would sense their absence and rush outside to cuff them back to the safety of the den. The young fisher usually complained until she boxed his ears. Afterward, he would grumble himself to sleep.

By the middle of their third month, she became more tolerant. Soon they were out to play for an hour or two each day, but always in the evening, and always under her watchful eye. They played games, dozens of them, kitten games like chasing beetles, hide and jump, leapfrog, wrestling, and a kind of raucous tag. But the young fisher's favorite was the stalking-springing game, where he would creep with splay-footed determination behind the low screens of ground cherry clumped about the entrance to the den, and spring with youthful savagery on the first of his family to come near. His mother looked on with approval. At times, when she pointedly was staring the other way, he would stalk her and spring ferociously on her tail with a high squeak that brought the other three cascading down to the attack.

When half of July had ticked away, the mother fisher began to grow increasingly serious and only grunted when the young fisher tried to gambol with her. She watched the moon, waiting till it waxed and lit the shadows with its fullness. Then on a night when the stars hung like frozen teardrops, she called her kittens to her. Muttering a signal to follow, she trotted slowly lakeward. The four, hushed and trembling with excitement, came after. The little female stopped to swat the half-closed, purplish blossoms on a tall, large-leaved aster. Her mother turned and swatted her.

For there was no time to waste. By October, by the time the geese flew south, she would have to teach them what they must know to live. To live alone.

* * *

I

In the gray dark of a hunter's moon, the mother fisher led her brood along the eastern shore of the lake. Occasionally, she glanced behind to see if they were keeping their proper stations. They had come far in the eight weeks since their first wild and hilarious hunting foray. Now they slipped in disciplined quiet through the classroom of the night. Yet, for all their stealth, the hushed night sounds died at the moment of their passing, to whisper forth again when they had gone. They moved as in a soft cocoon of tiny silences. Beneath the densest firs the light was very dim, but to the young fisher's night-seeing eyes, dimness was more comforting than day. Besides, the warm night breeze was alive with fascinating smells.

The young fisher's sister made the first kill in the cotton grass near the water's edge. The frog was still alive, though paralyzed, when she came proudly back to the shelter of the trees. They tore it apart, sharing the morsel with remarkably little fuss, though it only took the edge from their hunger. The mother fisher sat to one side, ready to cuff the first to start a fight.

The young fisher made the second kill, freezing at the sound of a faint rustle from a clump of northern maidenhair fern. He gave a throaty, meaningful grunt that stopped the others and crept forward to within springing distance. His leap was one his mother had recently taught them—a fluid, flashing dive to the right of the target. He screeched as he hit, twisted like a steel spring, and launched himself in a low, flat arc at a right angle to his first leap. It worked perfectly. The terrified rabbit had a sense of something dark above him as he shot from the ferns, but by then it was too late. This time the mother joined in sharing the warm, sweet flesh.

Now the mother fisher turned and led them inland, as she had for the past three nights, ever since the evening the men and dogs had arrived. The young fisher still remembered creeping with his mother and the others to within a hundred yards of the camp and crouching in the middle branches of a spruce, staring past the campfire toward the tall men and the two powerful dogs. The memory still intrigued him and once more, as he had the previous night, he whimpered to his mother and looked lakeward, asking that they go again. But despite her own intense curiosity, she would take no chances with four young kittens, and so she merely grunted and stalked away. The young fisher followed, fussing mightily.

Since the coming of the men, she had taken her young around the camp each night in a wide semicircle. She had made it plain that they were not to hunt until they were safely out on the north shore of the lake again. But on this night it was she who broke the rule, for quite suddenly, through the still darkness, she heard the keening of a porcupine. They were directly opposite the camp at the time, easing through the underbrush, but the sobbing wail sent her racing up an overgrown deer trail. The four kittens tumbled after.

The young fisher was the first to reach the moonlit clearing where his mother held the porcupine at bay. It was the first time he had seen such a creature and, as they had been taught, he and the others sorted themselves into a line to see how their mother would deal with it. It was a bulky beast, and though it likely weighed little more than she, the coarse, black fur, the bristling quills, and the humped back seemed to make it tower above her crouched litheness. She moved around the animal cautiously, one eye on the barbed tail, while she studied the lie of the clearing where they circled.

The clearing had come into being a half dozen years before, when the collapse of an elderly spruce had driven most of the younger growth to the ground. As a result it was long, nearly forty feet, and very narrow, hemmed in on one side by the deep-sweeping branches of younger spruces, and on the other by the jumble of the fallen trunk and broken, crumbling boughs.

The porcupine was angry, terribly so, for he held it his right to walk the northern woods without interference, and the sleek animal blocking his way was going against all established patterns. He grew steadily more exasperated. He grunted and angrily, impatiently began to stamp his little feet. The mother fisher paid him no heed, and slowly it began to dawn on him that he might be in extreme danger. He made efforts to reach a tree, but she headed him off, patiently working him toward the fallen logs in an awkward, stumbling circle, his quills bristling and chattering as he tried to keep his barbed and twitching tail always in her face.

It took her nearly ten minutes to herd the furious porcupine into position, but finally, when he was close to the weathered wood, she drew back to attack. When she moved, her leap was almost too fast to follow. Suddenly, she was beside the porcupine and then she was back, the only sound a faint swish and thud as the porcupine's tail lashed through the air and whacked the rotting wood. As the tail flicked back the young fisher saw that a dozen quills had been left in the log. Once more the mother fisher flashed in, and again, until the punky wood had collected a heavy fur of needle-sharp quills while the porcupine's club was nearly stripped of its armor. Then, with a movement a shade too fast to be casual, she dodged past the useless tail, slipped her nose beneath the shoulder of the bewildered animal and neatly flipped him over. She tore out his throat with a practiced slash and stood back to wait. Twice he screamed, high and mournfully. Then the tail thudded into the log, and he was gone. The mother signaled her kittens forward to eat. It was the most deliciously sweet and tender meat the young fisher had yet tasted.

But he had time to savor barely a mouthful when, with a crashing of brush, two dogs burst into the far end of the clearing. The mother fisher sprang to her feet with an indrawn hiss that sent her young scurrying beneath the spruce branches. Cautiously, the young fisher slipped forward and peered out. His mother was standing before the porcupine's carcass, snarling her fury at the intruders, her back arched, fur bristling, and her eyes blazing with a green glow. The dogs stopped, disconcerted, growling tentatively at the backs of their throats. They had been drawn from the camp by the first childlike wail of the porcupine and had lumbered through a night filled with animals that fled from their approach. Now they stood in a clearing that stank of blood, faced down by a slender creature smaller than either of them. It was a complete reversal of all they knew.

The Irish setter broke first and, with a bellow, charged down the clearing. The mother fisher leaped to meet his attack, moving slowly till she was nearly to him. She swerved as if to make for the trees, and the setter flew into a wild turn to head her off. Unexpectedly, she cut back in a sinuous jump and bore in at his unprotected side. The impact of her slight body tumbled him and shocked him so badly he did not really feel the gash her fangs had opened in his shoulder. Confused but still determined, he staggered to his feet in time to see her leap for the furrowed trunk of a tall, high-crowned spruce. He hit the tree three feet behind her, reached up and raked a rain of shaggy bark from the trunk. He shook the gritty crumbs from his eyes and reached up again. And then he froze, jolted to see her racing headfirst down the trunk at the same bewildering speed with which she had climbed it. The setter jerked back and dropped. His forepaw hit a root and he stumbled slightly.

The mother fisher hit screaming, slamming down onto his shoulders. He yelped and went down, his legs buckling, and before he could recover, she had buried her fangs into the back of his neck. He felt a sharp stab of pain and a terrible sense of pressure; then with a noise so immense it ravaged his ears, he heard the bone crunch and shatter. Within seconds he was dead. The fisher turned toward the second dog.

The Chesapeake Bay retriever was far from a coward, but his training was to retrieve, not attack. And now the sight of his companion, dead with such swift finality, unnerved him completely. He turned and fled. The fisher did not bother to follow. She stood listening to his crashing flight as the rage faded slowly from her eyes. Then she called her kittens to her.

Subdued, but excited at what they had seen, they crept from beneath the spruce boughs. They bunched together, trembling, as their mother led them to inspect the dead setter. The alien scent made their hackles rise, but dutifully, as she had taught them, they sniffed until the odor was firmly imprinted in their memories. Each tasted the strong, salty blood as if performing some ritual. The young fisher knew by the heavy flavor and scent that the dog was a meat eater but, like his mother, snorted disdainfully and trotted over to finish the delectable feast of porcupine.

He awoke shortly before the hot September sun reached the zenith. The liquid rays were spread across the mouth of the den, filling the musky air with a glow of dancing dust. The young fisher was curled in a ball with his brothers and sisters, drinking in the warmth and rich odor of his mother's flank. He was supremely happy, for he loved the den and the family. Only one thing marred this perfect day. His bowels were demanding relief.

Normally, he relieved himself in the late afternoon or early evening, but after the feast of porcupine, his body was demanding early action. With a grunt he rose and slipped out of the den. He paused on the shelf of granite before the entrance and tested the onshore breeze. It held the north in its arms, a subtle blend of growth, of life and death, of cool water and moist shadows and sunlight blazing on prehistoric rock, and through it all, like a recurring theme, the pungent smell of evergreen. High above the lake, an osprey swept on silent, circling wings, waiting for a fish to rise and furrow the surface of the waters. The young fisher watched its flight, then blinked happily and flowed downwind off the rock toward the friendly green gloom of the forest. The direction he took was different from that of yesterday. And yesterday he had taken a different direction from the day before. Each day throughout his life he would choose a different spot to bury his body's wastes, for he was a cautious and fastidious animal and would neither foul his own den nor leave a spoor that could point a revealing finger toward his refuge.

It was after he had finished and was conscientiously scraping the black loam over the hole he had pawed beneath the dense, overlapping fans of northern maidenhair fern that he saw the man.

Intuitively he crouched and froze. The man was

standing in the sunlight, a quarter of a mile away, staring up at the lichened rocks that tumbled in a frozen cascade from the old spruce to the water's edge. The Chesapeake Bay retriever was close to his heels, nervously following the man's every move as he picked his way up the weathered granite. Every few moments, at a word from the man, the dog moved ahead to nose out the trail. But the moment he found it, he would bark, then slip back to the hunter's side. The young fisher pressed back when they came abreast of him and bristled at the mingled odors sweeping toward him on the shifting breeze. The dog scent he recognized immediately from the night before. It did not disturb him too deeply. It was the other odor, the sharp, unanimal rankness and sweat smell of the man that raised his hackles. He narrowed his eyes against the glare and studied the strange, two-legged creature, memorizing every move, every scent and sound, for he knew with the cold, atavistic awareness of his predator's brain that it was in the man, not the dog, that the greatest danger lay.

They were scarcely fifteen feet from the screened entrance of the den, when the retriever jerked into a partial point toward the old, furrowed spruce and barked. Even the fisher could hear the change of tone, the suppressed, eager excitement in the single sound. Slowly, the man unlimbered his rifle and levered a cartridge into the breech.

A flight of buffle-heads arrowed swiftly across the lake, flying low to the water. The blink of sun on their white wing flashes momentarily caught the young fisher's eye. When he looked back the man was brushing aside the thick, low-growing ground cherry masking the den mouth. Though he was thirty feet away, the young fisher could hear his mother's sibilant, warning snarl. The man stepped back and began to cast among the gnarled roots of the huge, old tree, collecting handfuls of needles, broken, resinous branchlets, and sun-dried sedge. Two jays fluttered the limbs above him, cocking their bright blue, crested heads and hectoring with their incessant double-noted, nasal clicks while he pyramided the tinders in the center of the sticky-haired leaves. At the first wisp of smoke, they fled screeching up the shore of the lake. The man was so intent he scarcely seemed to hear them go. Nor did he see the young fisher when he strode toward the woods for fronds of rattlesnake fern to throw on the fitful, smoldering blaze.

The pitch of the mother fisher's snarls was rising. The young fisher tensed, wondering if he should join her. He looked at the man, standing near the den, then at the dog, poised and alert beside him. Regretfully, he eased back, knowing he must wait for her to show him what he must do. But it was the man who made the first move.

Impatiently, he whipped the peaked cap from his head, and tried to waft the stinging smoke into the den. It was the move the mother fisher had been waiting for. She was already clear of the ground and arching upward when she hit the den's entrance, teeth bared and a scream of hate and challenge in her throat. She went straight for the man's jugular, but in the blinding smoke she missed by a critical inch and caromed off his shoulder, spinning him half around while her teeth carved a jagged gash in his cheek that showed the white glint of bone before blood filled the wound. She landed accurately poised on her toes, half-turning to go back at him. The dog lunged to stop her.

The mother fisher sprang at the new target, but her swing toward the man had put her off the mark. She tried to snake her fangs down to the dog's throat as she flew past, but only succeeded in taking off most of an ear. The dog squealed, and in a frantic scrabble of claws, tried to turn on the slippery rock. He had no chance. She took out his jugular with a slash so swift her head barely seemed to flicker. The dog dropped like an empty sack.

The killing of the animal took possibly ten seconds, but they were seconds that cost the mother fisher her life. The man was ready for her, balanced on the balls of his feet, his rifle clubbed and swinging. The flat of the butt caught her in the ribs, crushing one side of her chest and driving the shattered bones into her lungs. The terrible force behind the blow drove her back six feet, tumbling her on the rock. She lurched forward again, determined in the face of her agony to save her young. She was still trying to reach the man when he fired the heavy-caliber bullet that killed her.

The roar of the shot echoed across the lake and back. From the den came growls and the sound of scrambling claws as the larger of the young fisher's brothers burst through the smoke, snarling and coughing.

Dazed by the fumes, blinded by tears, he tried vainly to find a target to attack, but before he could move the man was on him. The young fisher flinched as he heard the heavy rifle butt crush his brother's skull. The man jammed the muzzle into the entrance beneath the spruce, jabbing viciously at the two kittens inside. Swearing, he fired the carbine, ejected the shell, and fired again. The second blast blew a cloud of dust and loose bark into his face. He jerked away, rubbing his eyes.

Then painfully, blindly, the young fisher's sister dragged herself from the mouth of the den. She was whimpering and dazed. Both her eardrums had been shattered by the terrible concussion, and threads of blood were trickling down the fur below her softly rounded ears. The man ripped out an oath as he raised his rifle above his head and brought it crashing down on her spine with such force the stock was split from end to end. The little female pulled herself up on her forelegs, snarled at him, and collapsed. The man, his face a mask of blood, stood frowning stupidly at his rifle. Unconsciously, he put his hand to his cheek, then pulled it away, startled to see so much blood. He glanced down at the limp body of his dog and nudged it with his foot. He sighed, shrugged hopelessly and turned away, his fingers slipping in the cascade of blood on his cheek as he tried to hold the edges of the gash together. Slowly, like a man who has lost much more than he can afford, the hunter shambled toward the water's edge.

The young fisher waited until the man had washed his face clear of blood and trudged out of sight before he crept cautiously toward the den. He went straight to his mother, whimpering faintly at her glazed eyes and the froth of blood around her mouth. He nudged her flank, still musky and warm in the hot sun, still with the softness and mother smell that he loved. But there was no response. About her, he could sense the aura of death. And suddenly, he knew she was gone from him and would never come back.

The air was heavy with the stink of blood and powder fumes and acrid, clinging smoke. He snorted the smells from his nostrils as he checked each of his family. Hopefully, the young fisher touched each body, sensing as he did so that it was in vain. Finally, he stalked over to the body of the dog and ripped its other ear off. Then, as he spat out the unpleasant fur, he felt rising in him a great desire to get away, to leave this place. He did not look back as he melted into the soothing shadows of the cool, green forest.

He was a mile away when the fire started.

2

For nearly twenty minutes an unreal and brooding stillness hung in the air before the abandoned den, a hush so penetrating that the calls of the distant ducks and the rattle of the nearby jays had a strange thinness, a far-off, tinny sound, muted and obscured. Among the blood-soaked rocks there was only sun and silence, pierced now and then by the sharp, stinging buzz of muscid flies and bluebottles reaping the rich, red harvest.

Nothing happened immediately. The smudge the man had built smoldered fitfully, marked by a wispy, blue plume that stood straight up in the heavy air. A few, faint tendrils curled upward from the embers. A spark jumped from ember to rotted wood, glowed a moment, then faltered, slowly losing headway.

From the spruces near the lake there came the soft whisper of needle brushing needle. A circling osprey set his wings at a sharper angle and swung about, riding the rising breeze. The first, delicate gusts reached the old spruce, roiled the smoke, and tore its slender plume apart. And in the punk of rotten wood the little dot became a crawling, red-eyed worm, then two, then three. The worms met and spread into a glowing band that marched hungrily toward a patch of sedge. For a moment the sedge seemed to resist, and then it burst into flame.

The flames were invisible in the brilliant air, but the rippling waves of heat showed how they advanced, wavered, surged out again, nearly died away, and at the final moment touched the tinder-dry, hairy gray twigs of a winter-killed heartleaf willow. It exploded into annihilation, sending a shower of orange sparks raining down. Abruptly, the willow bush collapsed, gusting a spurt of flames toward the low, sweeping boughs of a young fir. With a deep and throaty rush the entire tree flared into flame, and the first column of oily, stinging smoke was hurled skyward.

A flight of crossbills erupted from the stand of spruce next to the blazing fir in a bright confusion of rosy bodies and flashing black and white wings. Through them rocketed a half dozen tiny pine siskins, reaching for altitude. Like a slow chain reaction, the disturbance spread from bird to bird around the lake. A family of rudy-crowned kinglets fluttered across the air. A medley of warblers followed, black-polls and magnolias and black-throated greens, their butterfly-bright swarms punctuated by the solemn shapes of juncos, grackles, and a single, huge and stately raven. From the shore a pair of mallards hit the sky, then bitterns, coots and green-winged teals, a family of yellow rails, another of mergansers, their slender, hooked bills agape with frightened, anxious cries. A pair of beautiful red-necked grebes swam in wide circles through the shallows, puffing out their white throat and cheek flashes in alarm, and shattering the afternoon with a chorus of brays and cacklings as they called their fledglings to them. Like most of the rest, they took to the air, then spiraled down to the water, becoming part of the vast winged ballet swirling above the lake. Nervous and apprehensive, they, like the others, were torn between wanting to escape and the need to stay a little longer at the nesting grounds.

In those first moments after leaving the arena where his family had died so brutally, the young fisher had trudged westward around the foot of the lake, then turned north to a clearing he remembered from a solitary afternoon's exploring a week before. His mother had come searching for him and had sent him flying home. Whether that was why he came, or because the clearing held such peace within the circle of its guardian pines, he did not try to understand. Instead, he simply trotted through the high, sweet, rustling bracken, looked about to choose a tree, then went fifty feet straight up to the cone-shaped crown of a slim jack pine.

He did not feel sorrow, for he was incapable of an emotion born from brooding on what might have been. What he did feel was much deeper, much more basic. He was possessed by a vast sense of emptiness that only his maturing body's readiness for a solitary life kept from becoming the ache of loneliness. The anger that had bubbled through him during the violence before the den began to seep away, fading from the short-lived red of rage to the deeper, lasting black of hate for the man and the man shape. For a little while, emotions foamed and bubbled through him, until the stillness around him soothed his body. He dropped his head to the furrowed bark, hooked his claws in a grip that nothing could break, then dropped the shutters across his soft black eyes and slept.

The clatter of the birds aroused him. He came awake with the all-encompassing awareness of a highly capable predator, instantly attuning his senses to the subtlest nuances of his environment. The birds were nervous, he could tell that immediately, and not only the transient, early migrators, but resident birds as well. Nor was this the anxiety of one family or two under siege from a fox or mink; he knew something larger must be afoot to send whole flocks fluttering indecisively into the sky.

He narrowed his eyes against the brilliance of the afternoon, peering through the screens of evergreen to where the birds rose and fell. He glanced at the molten sun. He inhaled the gusting breeze. It was bland and pleasant, filled with September's daytime smells. Everything was peaceful. Except the birds. Watchfully, the fisher slipped down to the lower branches of the pine.

An emphatic, muffled drumming rose from the clearing below. The fisher swept his eyes around the circle of trees and fastened on a tiny deer mouse. The little creature was perched on a rotting stump, so overgrown it was barely visible beneath the bracken. As the fisher watched, the mouse beat another swift tattoo with minute white feet against the weathered wood, then suddenly swung about, dropped into the bracken, and disappeared. Within minutes she was back, a squirming, downy shape gripped carefully in her mouth. She skittered up the stump, peered about cautiously, then dropped from sight into its hollow heart. Almost immediately she was out again, alone, and scurrying back across to the trees.

A faint but perceptible smell of burning began to filter into the clearing as the little deer mouse made trip after trip, determinedly moving her young to the new nest. Though her changing the nest was not in itself strange, her chancing it in the glare of day disturbed the fisher deeply. For he, like all animals, lived by inherent patterns of behavior, and living by patterns, he recognized them in others. For the mouse to expose her litter to daylight meant that a foe much more dangerous than her traditional enemies was driving her.

Quite suddenly, something took place that in the young fisher's eyes was so unusual that it brought him to his feet with every hair along his backbone bristling. The mouse, scurrying too quickly, dropped one of her young in the middle of the clearing. She dodged back to pick it up. At the same instant, the rusty shape of a long-eared owl detached itself from the wall of the pines and floated, blinking in the unaccustomed daylight, across the hazing air. The mouse and the owl were both in the open. Each saw the other clearly. Each had ample maneuvering room. Yet the mouse scarcely looked up, and the owl hardly looked down. And the fisher came down the pine in a single, fluid movement, determined to discover what was wrong.

The breeze and the terrain shaped the pattern of the fire at first, transmuting it from a perfect ring around the blazing fir to an amorphous, abstract shape that flowed along the lines of least resistance. It reached the southern shore of the lake and began a slow march eastward, struggling across ground that was low and damp, hindered by trees heavy with moisture. To the west, the advance was stopped completely by forty feet of bare granite framing the mouth of the small stream that fed the lake. But to the south, the flames found easy tinder. The breeze helped. Gusting off the lake, it drove the blazing perimeter along one bank of the stream, beating at the flames, trying to force them across toward the stony ridge that circled to the south and west.

A mile and a half upstream, the fire reached an elderly tamarack standing above the smaller, darker evergreens. A tongue of flame reached out and touched its autumn-yellowed needles, and in an instant it shot up to wreathe the crown, transforming the tree into a blazing, seventy-foot torch. The great tree shuddered along its length and toppled, thundering earthward to create a burning bridge across the stream. The crown crashed into the timber on the far bank, giving the fire the release it sought. Now the holocaust was no longer in the hands of the breeze. A gale could not have turned it from its course, for it was creating its own wind, sucking giant draughts of air in from every side, greedily devouring the oxygen it contained, then spewing the remainder upward in a column of writhing gases and oily smoke that drew a dingy veil across the sun.

The fisher picked his way along a jetty of rock that poked like a petrified finger toward the heart of the lake. For the first time since he left the clearing, the sun was dazzling, pouring with brassy insistence along his spine. Above, the sky was clear. Then the young fisher heard the sound, the deep, baying beast sound of the fire. His eyes snapped to the eastern shore, toward the gray smudge he first had thought was a bank of mist. Now he saw that where tendrils of gray writhed among the trees, the orange tongues of flames followed. To the south, the shoreline and all beyond were lost in a pall of smoke.

The fisher knew his danger now. Or rather, he knew he was in danger, without comprehending fully what the danger was. For a moment he contemplated taking to the lake and swimming northeast. But he had never been fond of water. He glanced back to where the tall firs spilled down to the lake. There was no smoke, at least none showing above the line of trees. Decisively, he turned and trotted into the comfort of the forest. He struck due west, but before long began a slow curve southward, drawn perhaps by the memory of the security he had once known in a den at the end of the lake.

Five minutes later, the first flames marched up the lakeshore to the jetty, where the fisher had stood. The fire's progress among the spruces south of the jetty had been swift, but it was nothing to the way the flames leaped through the stands of fir that lined the shoreline north. It was matched, a mile and a quarter to the west, by the blaze howling along the bone-dry crest of the ridge. Only in the corridor between was the fire's progress slowed, held back by deadfalls and the small, marshy clearings that pocked the forest, creating natural firebreaks.

It was pure, destructive force on the rampage, mindless and unselective. Yet, by the time it roared past the jetty, it had mindlessly built a trap that would destroy thousands of lives, terribly and soon. The young fisher was directly between the jaws.

3

It did not take the fisher long to sense he was moving in the wrong direction. As he neared the bracken-filled clearing he was surprised to meet the little deer mouse, racing through the haze with an infant in her mouth. Within minutes, he found himself traveling counter to a steady flow of animals, all heading in panicky determination for the lake. Bewildered, the young fisher watched creatures that were natural enemies pass within inches of each other. Even the infinitely timid snowshoe rabbits abandoned the safety of the thick undergrowth for the speed of the open trails, sparing scarcely a glance for the weasels and foxes fleeing beside them. A family of skunks passed him, mother and five striped kits, running flat out with their tail plumes low to the ground. Then a porcupine, a yearling with his black fur bristling and his quills rattling. Suddenly, the trees above were filled with screeching, frightened red squirrels, flying through the branches without a thought for the hawks. It took the fisher a second to realize why. There were no hawks. There were no birds at all. In the space of a minute, the screaming flocks had fled. He cocked his ears about. All he heard were frightened animals, and nearer now, a huge and rushing sound.

Suddenly he found himself surrounded by a new

wave of panicked animals, flooding away from the lakeshore. Perplexed, he paused with his senses taut for the first sign of something recognizably stable in a suddenly confusing world. When it came, it caught him unawares. An immense crashing surged up from southward, moving with startling speed. He swerved, teeth bared and ready, blinking away the stinging tears that threatened to blot out the vision of an enormous moose ploughing through the brush. He was a superb animal in the full glory of his breeding prime. But now his majesty was dimmed by the look of stark fear in the eyes, the flaring nostrils, and the dark streaks of sweat and foam marking his heaving flanks.

The fisher barely had time to leap aside as the great, splayed hooves thundered past. Impulsively, he whirled around, and at a dead run, fled north after the racing moose. He did not stop to think why he did, or even why he should. But as the moose went past, the fisher realized that the big creature was what he had unconsciously been searching for—an older and more experienced animal moving in one definite direction.

The moose, though he was capable of slipping his half-ton bulk and six-foot antlers through the woods like a gray-legged wraith, was crashing through them now, careless of how much noise he made. The fisher loped steadily after, but within a quarter mile, began to feel the pace. His lungs were laboring against the awful sting and burn of the stinking air. He tried to snort the gagging fumes away, to pace his breathing to the patches where the haze was thinner and less biting, but it did little good.

The moose crashed away. The fisher let him go, for he knew the direction he was traveling now. The south was hopeless, the streams of fleeing animals showed him that better than his own ears. To east and west the beast roar of the fire was solid and coming closer. To the north, although he could not really tell, the fire sounds seemed to be more hesitant, one moment whispering of a gap, the next shouting down the hope. The young fisher gave up and raced to the north, for he suspected that the pocket he was in was growing dangerously small.

He was right. The shore and the ridge fires were scarcely a quarter mile apart. Already they were at the stream that drained the northwest corner of the lake and were racing along its bank. The flames had finally overcome the hurdles to the south and had roared up from the bottom of the corridor until they were only a half mile from the juncture of lake and stream. There, the narrow mouth of the pocket was drawing swiftly together. The fire was only minutes away from obliterating everything within the tortured circle, and the fisher was still in its center, with a quarter mile to go.

He was on the move again, racing along a well-marked deer trail that pointed north as straight as a compass. But then it was gone, lost in murky smoke. Choking and gasping, the fisher scrambled wearily into the trees, resting until the dizziness eased and the ringing in his head subsided. He lurched into action again in a series of fantastic leaps that took him through the close-grown trees as swiftly as he could move along the ground.

Suddenly, and with numbing speed, the fire crowned. The fisher plunged wildly earthward seconds before the holocaust swept toward him through the tops of the trees. He was surrounded by flame. His ears rang from the violent crash of blasted timber as the awful dome of fire began to eat downward. He could scarcely see through the tears cascading from his eyes. Time and again he blundered across the bodies of smaller animals dying in the suffocating heat.

Unexpectedly, he burst into a clearing. One wall was half ablaze, the other solidly aflame. Toward the north end, the fisher sensed an alleyway between the trees and beyond it the suggestion of a glint of water. He vaguely made out six wavering tamaracks, still standing black against the flames. Their crowns were blazing torches, but the lower trunks were holding out, keeping a narrow corridor momentarily free from flame. The fisher stumbled on. He was beyond thinking, beyond decision. Instinct alone drove him toward the only dark spot in a seething, orange world. And suddenly, miraculously, the air was clear. Overhead, the ceiling of flame was eating such vast quantities of oxygen that it sucked a stiff breeze of cool, moist air from the water ahead. It blew with a force close to gale along the narrow corridor, washing it free of smoke and falling sparks. To the young fisher, it was a stimulant. He filled his shuddering lungs with huge draughts of wonderful coolness. He shook his head frantically to clear his eyes and peered blearily ahead. The edge of the forest was only thirty feet away, and beyond it was a shelf of striated granite that dropped in shallow steps to the beckoning surface of the stream. With a scurry of scrambling claws, the fisher raced for the safety of the open air.

He nearly made it.

Thirty feet downstream from the edge of the granite, a mature balsam fir was in the last moments of its life. It was pure coincidence that the instant the fisher reached the granite was the instant the trunk ripped violently apart. The fisher heard the blast and, almost immediately, felt something falling across his shoulders. Abruptly he was writhing on the ground in a rain of falling debris. A flying gout of sticky resin had splashed across his shoulders, driving deeply into his fur. The burning liquid laid a saddle of fire across his shoulders, crisping his fur and blistering the skin beneath. Snarling and screeching, he wrenched his head back to bite at the clinging mass, but he only burned his delicate nose and tongue.

The pain sent him staggering toward the edge of the granite shelf. Scarcely conscious, he thudded down the steps and into the stream. Spluttering, he struggled up from the depths and tried to sneeze the water from his nose. Gradually, it was borne upon him that he was out of the terrible fire. Slowly, as his mind crept out of shock, he found that the coolness of the stream was washing the pain from his shoulders.

For the first moments he swam strongly, kicking out with all four limbs against the sluggish current. Then, waves of weakness began to wash through his body. Moment by moment, the strength in his forelegs seeped away, and he was conscious of pain again. Not the agony of the resin, but a deeper, duller ache that sapped his shoulder muscles of their power. Wracked by smoke, blasted by heat, and shocked by burns, his young and vibrant body was beginning to fail. For all his youth, the fisher knew with a frightening certainty that if he did not soon find rest, he would die.

Paddling with his hind feet, his forepaws curled beaver-like against his chest, he swam in a narrow circle through the water, searching for anything to take his weight. The stream was filled with debris, shattered branches and slabs of bark, most of it much too small. He felt a nudge against his shoulder and yelped, kicking away from what had touched him. A huge, dark shape turned and rolled in the eerie, bloodshot light. It was the shattered crown of a magnificent fir, reduced by fire to a blackened log. He lunged toward it and with a last, hidden reserve of strength, heaved himself aboard.

The wood was steaming slightly. He felt the log tilt crazily under his weight, but he dug in his claws, shifting his bulk to keep the refuge upright. Straining to hold his balance, he worked his way forward, fighting through waves of nausea and dizziness to reach a small crotch, framed by the charred stumps of several branches. Painfully, wearily, the fisher dragged himself into the hollow of the crotch, and locked his claws deeply into the wood in a grip that not even death could break.

He did not feel the blasts of heat that struck at him from either bank. He did not know he gagged and coughed when low coils of smoke clawed at his throat. And when the rain came, it was only a steady, cold drumming across his blistered back.

4

THE OLD OJIBWAY spotted the fire early in the afternoon while harvesting the small stand of rice growing in the marshy shallows of his lake. Stretching to ease his back from the labor of kneeling in his canoe, he let his eyes roam the tree line. They stopped and hardened at the suggestion of a faint, blue-gray smudge to the southeast. With long, powerful strokes that seemed unlikely in a man of so many years, he drove the canoe out of the swaying stems, swept around the promontory across from the clearing where his cabin stood, and angled sharply toward the southernmost shore. He swung into a natural dock between two jagged piers of granite, then trotted with catlike grace toward a dim game trail.

The trail wavered upward, zigzagging across a long slope and past a jumble of rocks and berry bushes to the foot of a steep ridge, which climbed high enough to overlook the entire lake. From the pinnacle, a single black spruce soared skyward. The old Indian was breathing heavily by the time he reached it, but he swung into the branches, climbing steadily toward a sturdy, well-worn limb, forty feet up. Brushing the needles and crumbs of bark from his shirt, he settled against the trunk and narrowed his eyes toward the southeast.

Though distance masked the details, he could see the fire was growing rapidly. From a few, indistinct puffs, it had burgeoned to a massive column, a quarter mile across and at least a mile high. As he watched, he saw it change again, broadening into a long, ominous band that told him it was surging through extremely flammable timber. He judged the fire had started at the south end of the next lake, and that the main advance was north along the high ground between the two lakes. That, at least, would give him a few minutes' grace before he would have to leave the heights and start to strip his cabin. He closed his eyes painfully, vizualizing the havoc the fire would bring, the terrible red destruction, the appalling loss of life. And afterward, the gray and black of total devastation.

He had a fair idea of who had started the blaze, though not of how or why. In a way, he blamed himself. Three days ago, two hunters had come to his lake with dogs and a good canoe filled with sparkling equipment. He knew the type well. Hunters, and likely not bad hunters at that, but certainly not woodsmen. Men who came to the woods for a few weeks each year, who knew all the rules by rote and so were capable of immense stupidities. He knew them because he had guided their kind for years. And wanting his lake to remain peaceful and untouched, he had indulged himself to the extent of convincing them that the game around the virgin lake six miles upstream would give them far better sport. Now, the woods around that lake were burning. He cursed himself for a selfish fool.

But he was so sick of the white man.

The breeze gusted, and the old man began to feel a faint glimmer of hope as he looked up to the dancing crown of the tree. There was no doubt, the wind was freshening. His eyes took in the vast sweep of clouds smothering the northern horizon, so still all day, but now boiling closer. His pulse began to quicken. From years of watching the play of changing seasons he knew that the last big thunderstorm of the year was likely in the making, that far to the north a river of dry, brisk polar air was pushing the clouds before it, laying down a band of rain that could be anywhere up to a hundred miles in depth. He could only hope, and perhaps pray, that it would reach the fire before the fire reached him.

Scarcely thinking of what he did, the old Ojibway took his pipe from his pocket, lit it, and blew a puff of smoke to the four points of the compass. He was rather amused to catch himself at this, for it was his people's way of making a gentle offering to the frog spirit, the bringer of rain. He toyed with the idea of climbing down from his perch to find a snake, and then to kill it and stretch it belly up in the sun, for it was a sure and tested way to call the thunderbird from his rocky nest with eyes flashing lightning and wings beating thunder. Then he laughed at himself and, still grinning, said a Hail Mary for luck instead.

The flames were visible now, as a line of brilliant gold and orange between the sharp, black of the distant ridge and the roiled gray smoke above. He watched closely, hoping the fire would descend the near slope more slowly than it had climbed the far. He looked back to the thunderheads and saw with relief that the tenuous edge of the soft, gray strato-cumulus was beginning to haze the sun. For a last moment before the low-hanging clouds swept across the lake, he could still see the majestic, pearly anvils marching close behind, towering up thousands of feet into the intensely azure sky, each surrounded by a nimbus of plaited sunshine. Then the sun was gone. The lake turned from pewter to lead. The air took on an unreal, aqueous glow, a soft, submarine quality that rounded all edges while it sharpened all colors. As the first rain fell, the old Ojibway closed his eyes in gratitude and lifted his face to the huge, stinging drops.

The storm hit with a flash of lightning and a crash of thunder that split the air like an ax. The tentative, warning drops were drowned in a numbing sheet of rain. The old man hunched his shoulders and settled back to watch and wait. He knew perfectly well that he was in danger, sitting in the highest tree on the highest point of land in the middle of a monumental thunderstorm, but he was seventy years a fatalist and refused to deny himself the thrill of participating in one of the great spectacles of nature. Then a sundering crash shattered the air from somewhere behind. A hundred and fifty feet away, the compact crown of a jack pine lay shattered, tumbled halfway off the lower slope of the ridge. Thirty feet of the trunk was still standing, despite a gigantic, bleeding split where the lightning had cleaved it to the roots.

For an instant the air over the center of the lake

was swept clean, and he saw a forest of snapping, forked tongues dancing across the water, slashing down at the tops of the sullen, mounting waves. Abruptly the scene was gone, wiped away as a sudden gust trembled his tree and opened up a lane of clear air to the bay. There the waves were ordered, chopping viciously south, directly toward his moored canoe. With a shrug, the old man worked his way down the tree.

The cold front passed as he plunged into the woods, and he shivered at the swift drop in temperature. Beneath the trees, the rain poured down in rivers. He smiled, knowing that to the southeast, the same tiny torrents were killing the blaze more effectively than any man could hope to do.

The storm died as the old man knelt by his canoe to drain the rain water from his rice, and he looked up sharply, listening to the thunder rumbling away to the south. Overhead, clouds still stretched in an opaque, sunless veil, and he knew the pause was momentary, a hiatus between the passing of the thunderheads and the coming of a deep band of teeming drizzle. With a great, comforting rush, it swept across the lake, dropping straight through the dead calm air and beating down the tops of the choppy waves. As the lake stilled, he launched out, cutting across the mouth of the incoming stream toward his clearing.

He nearly missed seeing the fisher. At first, the tree crown carrying the unconscious animal was just one charred snag among many. Then he saw the irregular hump in the hollow of the branches and swung around to investigate. For a moment, seeing the sticky mass across the animal's shoulders, he considered tipping the log to give the creature the swift mercy of drowning. Then he slipped his fingers beneath the neck and felt the strong, slow pulse. Gently, he disengaged the claws from the wood and lifted the slender form aboard.

It was still pouring when the old Ojibway reached the cabin and carried the unconscious fisher inside. He kicked a pile of rice sacks into a corner near the stove and laid the animal on them. Working very carefully, he toweled the fur dry. The matted hair across the shoulders came out in charred lumps beneath his touch. Digging into his belongings, he found a seldom-used straight razor and cut the balsam-choked fur free. Then, with gentle fingers, he smoothed a layer of fat over the burn.

Consciousness came back to the fisher in a rush. Before the Indian was even aware, the animal turned and snapped. The old man stepped back chuckling, sucking a small gash on the heel of his hand. The fisher lurched to his feet with a screech of rage. For a moment he stood swaying, then his forelegs collapsed, and he fell gasping.

The old Ojibway was wise in the ways of animals. He had expected a reaction when the fisher woke, but not such a one as this. Fear perhaps, certainly a snarled warning, but nothing like the fury now flaring in the fisher's eyes. Somewhere, he must have come into violent contact with man. The animal was young, born last

March or April, and the only men in the area since then had been the hunters. Likely, the fisher had had some sort of run-in with them. Beyond that, the Indian could not begin to guess. Outside, the rain was beginning to let up, so he collected his drying pans and left the animal to calm itself.

Helpless, the fisher lay on the soft sacking, watching the old man as he went through the motions of transferring the rice to the round, flat pans. The man shape triggered the memory of the death in the clearing, and beyond it the choking of the smoke and the orange horror of the fire. He remembered the shock of the burn, the cool wash of the river, and the relief as the log steadied beneath him. After that—nothing.

Again he tried to come to his feet, but again slumped back, instinctively aware that to survive meant resting here until he was at least partly healed. His eyes told him that he was in a strange, enormous den, filled with things whose shape meant nothing to him. His nose was more productive, for he immediately recognized the tang of woodsmoke, the cold smell of iron, and, very faintly, the hint of gunpowder. There was an odor of cooking, and through it the scent of fresh meat and fur. The stench of the fat on his shoulder nauseated him, and he tried to remove it, but only managed a few licks before the pain stopped him. Over everything else, sharp and quite unmistakable, was the man smell, the rank stink that had struck so piercingly through the fire and iron and dog and blood smells before the old den. And yet, in this man shape there was a difference, a certain muskiness that robbed the odor of much of its sting. As if there were something of the animal in the man.

In a way the fisher was right, for the old Ojibway had literally returned to nature after a life spent mostly in the towns. Mission-raised and mission-school-educated, he had escaped at fifteen to the bawdy atmosphere of the logging camps in winter and the track gangs in summer. Spring was the time for general hell-raising, and the brief autumns for hunting. At twenty he met and married a loving girl with tender, laughing eyes. She had borne him two children before she died, killed by the extended labor of trying to give life to a third, a doomed infant who followed his mother within a day. His daughter was still alive, the wife of a Mohawk construction worker who followed the high steel across the country. His son had died early in the War.

Within a week of receiving the telegram, the old man had lied about his age and enlisted. Two months later he was in England, building airstrips. He saw part of the bombing of London, was sent to North Africa, to Italy, then back in time to be caught in the buzz-bomb and V-2 raids. And though he was inured to suffering and death, he found the blind, mindless destructiveness of the rockets too much to stomach. He was granted a transfer to a combat troop in time to take part in the invasion of Europe. He made sergeant, and was recognized by his officers as perhaps the best night reconnaissance patrol leader in the army, a scout who moved like a shadow and killed as silently as he moved. They never knew that behind his unemotional eyes was a growing sickness at a world where shedding blood seemed the only way of ending bloodshed.

At the end of the war, he came back to the lumber camps and track gangs. But spring was no longer a time for raising hell; instead, he wandered the north woods and found in the rebirth of the seasons a salve for the scars on his soul. He still hunted in the fall, but found there was little pleasure in the killing. His friends began to drift away, but that did not disturb him, for he was finding a new world among the creatures of the wild. Slowly, the urge was born to leave the life that had become so barren to him, to return to the great, green forest and the stillnesses that for so many centuries had birthed and nurtured his kind.

For the first time in his life he began to save. He hired out as a guide to fishing parties, to geological and survey groups, and in the autumn, to hunters. Impatiently, he watched his bank balance grow until finally, in his sixtieth year, he simply turned his back, and without a word of farewell, paddled north.

He chose his lake with care, in an area where the paucity of large rivers made logging operations economically unsound. The tiny stand of wild rice was an added bounty, since the extra money bought supplies that helped reduce the need to kill for food. Now he hunted only an occasional deer, a few rabbits and squirrels, the rare fox that disturbed his chickens, and all the nesting crows he could shoot. He knew a pair of nesting crows were capable of destroying fifty to a hundred songbird eggs daily, and he waged a constant war to drive them from his lake. Otherwise, he subsisted quite well on fishing, the supplies he trekked in, and the eggs from the three hens that lived beneath the eye of an old rooster in the small, sturdy run behind the cabin.

The fisher was asleep when he returned, but at the first touch of a foot on the floorboards, the wary, black eyes snapped open. The animal seemed resigned to his presence, only snarling when he passed close to the corner. As the man lit the stove, the fisher cringed, hissing at the flash of golden flame and the sharp sting of smoke. Softly, the old man crooned an Ojibway lullaby, and after several tense and watchful minutes, the fisher relaxed.

All through the long evening the fisher watched, puzzled and wary, but no longer seething with rage. He wrinkled his nose at the smell of cooking and coldly refused the piece of well-hung meat the old man pushed toward him with a stick. Later, he watched as the man stirred the pans of rice over a small drying fire just outside the cabin door. And finally, under the combined persuasion of the luxurious warmth and his own exhaustion, his head dropped. The delicately rounded ears cocked once as the weird, laughing yodel of a loon echoed across the evening, and then he slept.

Much later the old Ojibway found the fisher shivering in a feverish dream. Rummaging through a small pile of furs, he drew out a partially finished blanket made from long, interwoven strips of white snowshoe rabbit fur. He warmed it at the stove and spread it over the sleeping animal. The fisher snapped at him once, drowsily, then with a mumbling sigh that the old man found oddly touching, he burrowed his nose into the fur and drifted into a deep and healing sleep.

* * *

5

THE MAN WAS GONE when the fisher awoke. For a minute, he confused the cabin with the old den under the spruce, then memory rushed back, leaving him alert and wary.

Through the open door, he saw the old man at the shore, silhouetted against a background of such vivid color that the fisher mistook it for flame. But the peacefulness of the scene, the untroubled blue of the sky, the clarity of the breeze quelled the fear before it was fully born. He looked more closely and noticed tiny, bright-winged shapes flashing in and out and through the wall of color, and behind them, the bushy-tailed antics of squirrels. Abruptly, his eyes found the point of focus, and the brilliant mass broke up into separate trees, dressed in a flaming autumn glory he had never seen before.

The trees were the old man's hobby. Each autumn, when he took his annual trip to the trading post to sell his harvest and purchase supplies, the old Indian would roam for a day through the stands of hardwood, carefully choosing two or three sturdy young saplings to transplant to his lake. One by one, he cleared the cedars and spruces from the spit of land across the narrow bay; leaving only an outer fringe as a windbreak. Lovingly, he replaced them with his own trees. Now, every autumn, he savored the reward he had labored for, as, against a backdrop of evergreens, the flaming maples, the golden poplars, the rich, red oaks, and the buttery birches cast a riot of color across the calm water before his door.

The fisher tensed as the old man entered the cabin with one of the round drying pans. He snarled a warning. The old man answered in his quiet singsong and, kneeling just out of reach of the fisher's fangs, slid the pan into the corner. Then, picking up a fishing rod, he walked toward the shore.

The fisher inspected the pan. It was half filled with black loam overlaid with fronds of sweet-smelling bracken. Gingerly, grunting at the pain, he climbed in and relieved himself. The familiarity of the act left him feeling considerably better, well enough to make a first survey of this huge, den-like place. Slowly, he started on a circuit of the cabin. The bunk was thick with the smell of man so he skirted it with only a distasteful, bristling inspection. He separated the pile of furs in the corner into individual species by scent—the bland odor of rabbit, the sharper tang of fox, the nutty muskiness of squirrel. The rack of rifles beside the door brought a harsh growl to his throat, for the pungent mixture of oiled wood, of steel, and the ugly reek of powder held too many disturbing associations. He backed away, snuffling.

He found the other side of the door delightfully alive with the homey smell of wood. Beneath a low workbench were piles of cedar roots, creamy-white rolls of papery birch bark, hanks of threadlike tamarack roots, and slender bundles of grayish-purple willow branchlets. During the long, closeted winters the old man spent much of his time here, working on delicate paintings and carvings of the legendary figures of his tribe. His carefully stylized representations of thunderbirds and snake sturgeons and mermen had gained a certain popularity among dealers in primitive art far to the south. His commissions, though not large, helped maintain his bank balance.

The fisher snuffled happily among the aromatic cedar chips, inhaling the fragrance deeply. But enervating waves of weakness were flooding down from his shoulders, sapping his strength. He limped past the open, blackened maw of the fireplace, then slumped down on the fur and sacking, and dozed.

When the old man returned, the fisher was grooming his fur. The Indian's eyes softened as he watched the animal carefully untangling the snarls with his teeth. It obviously hurt the fisher to move, but the grooming instinct was stronger than the pain, and already the fur was beginning to gleam with the dark inner light that made fisher fur so prized. Very gently, the fisher started to wash his shoulders, spitting out the chunks of fur that came loose to reveal the massive blisters of ruddy, seared flesh of the burn.

The Indian unearthed one of his few dishes, dippered it full of water, and slid it in front of the animal.

The fisher gave a tentative sniff, an experimental sip, then began to lap greedily, humming with pleasure as the liquid flowed into his parched body. Next the old man reached into his fishing creel, lifting out a fat leopard frog. He killed it expertly, dismembered it, and pushed the bits toward the animal. The fisher turned the pieces over with his nose and nipped neatly into a meaty leg. He suddenly found himself ravenous. He ate steadily, crunching the bones with a certain daintiness when he was through. When he looked up, the man was cutting the thick back meat from a remarkably ugly burbot. Actually, it was the first fish the animal had ever seen, for despite the name, fishers perform poorly in the water.

The old man fed the fisher as much as he would eat, for he knew the animal was incapable of gluttony, that, like most predators, the fisher would never allow himself to overeat to the point where his speed and agility would be impaired. Then he deep-fried two burbot steaks for himself and left for the rice stand.

In the days that followed, the two slipped into a pattern of living that was to order their lives for the weeks ahead. It was an odd pattern, based not on trust, but a strangely tolerant mutual respect. The old Indian never touched the fisher, never came near him except in the evenings with food and water and in the mornings to change the pan of loam. For his part, the fisher stopped snarling whenever the man came near and, in time, even allowed himself to sleep while the Indian moved about the cabin. The fisher never indicated that he expected to be fed. Patiently, he waited for the old man to prepare their separate meals, then accepted what was offered with grave dignity.

The fisher's burn healed rapidly. Within a week, the blisters were subsiding. Another week, and the hardened tissue began to split and peel, showing the bright pink of tender, new skin beneath. The fisher groomed himself constantly, and soon the ravages of the fire were gone from his coat. Only the hairless welt across the shoulders remained. The old man knew how important it was to stop adhesions from forming, and as soon as the fisher showed signs of being able to move without too much pain, he began to bring live food for the animal to stalk. The fisher was clumsy at first, but as his shoulder muscles strengthened, he regained his old proficiency.

It fascinated the old man to watch him. The Ojibway people called the fisher "Black Cat," and watching the young animal, he could understand why. The fisher was remarkably feline in his way of moving and in his swift, precise spring toward his prey. But perhaps most of all, it was his catlike quality of intense concentration, his total involvement in whatever he was doing that the man admired most. The only time he saw the fisher lose his dignity was when he brought home a dozen crayfish and tipped them out on the floor. The fisher scarcely knew what to do first. He leaped among the scuttling creatures, grunting and yipping with delight, trying to flip them with his nose and paws. But of all the treats the old man offered him, it was the eggs he loved most. After two extremely messy, experimental tries, he learned to cradle them gently between his paws while he nipped the top off neatly. Sometimes, he would delight the old Indian by juggling the empty shell between his feet with such an air of grave playfulness the old man was forced to choke back his laughter. To let it out, he felt, might offend the fisher's dignity.

Meanwhile, autumn began its long, downhill slide to winter. Day by day, the sun marched in a lowering arc across the piercing, cobalt sky. The air was a sparkling wine, full of snap and brilliance. The nights grew chill. Yet, the afternoons were warm and lazy, still filled with summertime.

There was a mounting restiveness that communicated strongly to the fisher as he stretched out each afternoon, drinking in the warmth of the autumnal light sluicing across the open doorway. He felt it as he listened to the red squirrels hurling their valiant territorial challenges back and forth between the pines and spruces. All day and every day, they raced against the sun, trying to complete their harvest before the coaxing warmth burst the cones to scatter their papery seeds on the wind.

The shore and water birds moved with an air of tense expectancy. As the days grew shorter, the mysterious migratory urge was triggered, even among fledglings that had known no other world but the lake. All through the afternoon and every afternoon, the marsh would come alive as family after family of ducks would rise. First the pintails, only half out of eclipse plumage with breasts of white and backs of gray and with secondary wing flashes weaving patterns of violet and bronze and green across the sky. Whirling up, then zigzagging down, they would break away in a swift, whistling glide that skimmed them over the water for several hundred yards before they touched the silvery surface once again. As they settled, teals took over the dance. From behind the burr reeds, the chunky little soras fluttered weakly skyward, a solemn slate beside the formal dress of solitary sandpipers. The ploy-colored mallards winged noisily above them, while farther out the diving ducks, the ring-necks and golden-eyes and buffle-heads pattered across the water, leaving a momentary trail of rippling footprints as they literally ran into the air.

It was late one night in early October when the Canada geese came. The fisher awoke instantly at the distant, wild call and heard an answering echo in himself. The joyous notes of the high-winging, midnight singers struck a chord so sweetly it made his heart ache for the spruce-scented gloom of the forest and the thrill of a free, swinging chase through the treetops. It was time to leave, and knowing he would not return, he padded around the cabin to give each article a farewell sniff.

A second flight of geese, winging southward at a lower altitude, awakened the old man. He opened his eyes and smiled at the lonely music. Gradually, he became aware of the watching figure at his side. He turned his head. Bathed in moonlight from the window, the fisher was sitting on his haunches, staring as if to memorize the old Indian's face. The pale half-light gleamed on his fur, once more soft and dark and luxurious. A glowing band sat across his shoulders like a miniature saddle where the fur had grown through the burn scars, not dark and sleek, but a strange, ghostly white that would mark him to the end of his life. The old man felt a prickling in his scalp. How many nights had the fisher sat this way, watching him in sleep while the moonlight spread across his unprotected throat? How easy it would have been for the animal, and how swift.

Then, in the space of a blink, the fisher was gone. The Indian heard a rattle of claws on wood, and saw a crack of starlight materialize from the gloom around the door. A dark shadow slipped through and melted into the darker shadows of the night. For the first time in many years, the old man felt a great sense of loneliness.

6

THE FISHER stood before the cabin inhaling the night with deep and serene relish. An arrowhead of geese drifted across the face of the moon, their wings moving in easy rhythm as each rode the lifting vortex of air sculled back by the bird in front.

The air was chill without being cold, filled with a heady briskness that sent the blood singing vibrantly through the fisher's veins. Alert to every sound and movement, he worked south—across the stream and into the trees. Suddenly exhilarated, he took to the branches, losing himself in the glorious universe of height and space and swaying boughs. Then, as the terrain began to climb toward the ridge, he came to earth, impelled by the pressing need to find a den. He investigated several hollow stumps and logs, even went so far as to enter an old fox burrow, but disliked the exposed entrances of the first and was repelled by the rank odor of the second. Finally, he trotted up from the edge of the trees and walked along the spine of the ridge toward the tall, sentinel spruce. It was exactly the location he had been seeking.

The side of the ridge fell sharply toward the lake, dropping vertically till it met a long, slanting ledge of weathered granite. From the ledge, the ridge fell away for another twenty feet until it lost itself in the margin of bushes and trees. The ledge itself was narrow, almost inaccessible from above, but at the point directly below the spruce, the gnarled roots had forced their way into the rocks to form a steep but practical ladder. The fisher spotted it and swung over.

The ledge was crumbling along its outer edge, eaten away deeply by years of frost and rain. Hundreds of cracks lined the back wall, radiating from the western end where unimaginable years ago, a tremor had split the rock to its depths. Time had rounded the harsh edges of the split, and the years had brought an accumulation of debris that slowly moldered into loam and formed a soft earthen floor. Inside the narrow opening the weathering was much more extensive, for as the fissure had provided dens for generation after generation of animals, so had their breath provided the frost that crumbled the rock, creating a safe, roomy chamber.

The fisher entered cautiously. The den was empty, but only recently so, for the smell of an animal clung strongly to the walls and floor. He tried to locate the scent in his memory, but it was new, from an animal he did not know.

He set about making the den his own. In the farthest corner was a scattered pile of rabbit bones. He inspected them, one by one, carried them outside and dropped them from the far end of the ledge. Then he worked over the ground, raking and turning it with his claws until the alien animal odor was drowned in the redolent bouquet of fresh earth. Satisfied at last, he stretched and yawned with a proprietary air before he fitted himself into the freshly burrowed hollow.

The first, pale hint of light was framing the entrance when he awoke and sensed the animal. He lifted his head and cocked his ears forward. There was nothing, and then, faintly, a quiet questing sniff, followed by a sibilant hiss. The fisher rose to his feet, silently waiting. The light was tenuous, frail, and yet he caught the indication of a movement, a minute and shifting darkness on the granite. Then, the lynx looked inside.

They eyed each other coldly, measuringly. The lynx spat, a vicious hiss of breath that trailed into a wavering growl, high in the throat. Automatically, the fisher snarled an answer while he studied the beast before him. Its face seemed strange, unnaturally round with a flat, snoutless look he had never come across before in anything but man. Then, dimly, he made out the predatory muzzle and bared fangs, the black-barred ruff of whiskers, and tufted black-edged ears. They made a perfect frame for the startling eyes—eyes that gleamed with a slit-pupilled coldness.

What the lynx saw reassured her. The fisher looked scarcely half her size, so she hunched her shoulders, extended her claws and reached out an enormous, fringed paw. The fisher crouched and slashed, missing the oversized foot by a fraction of an inch. The lynx scrambled out of the entrance, and the fisher lunged. Automatically, the lynx struck.

It was not a strong blow, rather an exploratory pat.

But her claws were partly unsheathed, and they scraped across the burn scars on the fisher's shoulders. The skin was scarcely broken, but the pain was like a fuse to the fisher. With eyes like agates and a snarl that wavered up scale to a scream, he slid into a deadly and implacable advance.

The lynx spat tentatively, then withdrew along the entire length of the ledge, the spotted silver fur along her backbone bristling with anger and alarm. Finally, she could go no farther. She bunched against the laddered roots and struck. The fisher's reaction was so swift she barely saw it. He slipped under her flashing paw, twisted, then sprang, going straight for her throat. She jinked violently, felt the rotten rock crumble beneath her weight, and went over the edge.

Catlike, she twisted in mid-air and landed on her padded feet. Directly above, she saw the fisher plunge over the edge and come screaming headfirst down the cliff. The lynx swung about and raced for the thick brush edging the trees. Seconds later, the fisher reached the clump of squashberry and bracted honeysuckle through which she had plummeted. Everything was quiet, unnaturally quiet, without even a hint of the fleeing lynx. And yet, he was certain the dying night breeze was carrying a suggestion of her scent from straight ahead.

The lynx was barely twenty paces away. Crouched on the lowest limb of a young black spruce, she watched the fisher slip silently toward her, his senses concentrated on the ground. As he passed beneath, she launched out, aiming her heavy forelegs at the middle of his spine. The fisher caught the faint scrape of claws and leaped to one side. He heard her teeth snick chillingly on the empty air and felt a sharp jab of pain as the taloned paws, missing his backbone, raked the flesh of his flank.

He blundered into the spruce where she had crouched, and started spiraling up the trunk to safety, then reversed direction on the trunk and shot around to the side facing the lynx. She was not fast enough to dodge him; nothing could be but another fisher. But she was able to jerk her head far enough around to guard her throat before the impact of his body sent her staggering. The fisher's teeth closed on her thick ruff of whiskers. He caromed off, heaving her head back as the fur tore loose. She whirled, fighting to keep on her feet, and after one horrified, unbelieving glance raced away.

The fisher stopped a moment to spit out the soft fur, then set out in pursuit. At times he could hear the rustle of her passage ahead, so he could not conceive at first why she headed west and then began a slow swing southward. Suddenly, understanding burst over him. He knew with absolute certainty that she was on her way back to the ledge. He shot forward, careless of danger from above. Within seconds, he had reached the screened opening where the trail left the trees. He was just in time to see the flicker of silvery fur as she started up the slope.

He whirled and galloped along the margin of the trees, determined to reclaim the den before the lynx. He was a dark, molten streak in the pallid light, moving so swiftly that the few night creatures still abroad had no time to think of flight before he was past and gone.

The fisher reached the slope below the ledge and loped up it. The speed of his running start carried him to the first foothold, a small outcropping of frangible rock. Twisting sinuously, he set his claws against the lichen-covered surface and leaped in a violent diagonal toward a mat of evergreen cassiope sprouting from a cleft in the granite. It snapped and crumpled under the impact of his body, but held long enough for him to set his claws again and hurl himself elastically upward to sprawl over the rim of the ledge. With a slow, extremely powerful movement, he heaved himself up and lay panting on the smooth surface. Then he composed himself to face the lynx.

The fisher was on his feet and advancing when the lynx touched the ledge and turned. For a moment, she was sure she must be facing another animal, but the white saddle across the fisher's shoulders was unmistakable. She had no illusions about the fisher now. Though she had the advantage of weight, he had speed and ferocity greater than any she had ever seen. Here on the ledge, a fight could have only one conclusion. Unless she held the den.

She waited until he was halfway along the ledge before she sprang, shooting into a high, arching leap intended to take her over the fisher and into the den. But the fisher was all steel wire and reflexes, and as she left the ground, he lunged, twisting smoothly in mid-air to reach up and rake her rib cage with his fangs. She hit the ledge with a stagger that took her perilously close to the edge. The fisher took the opportunity to slip past into the den. The lynx spat once, laid her ears back, and went down the rock face to the slope below.

The fisher watched her go and was torn by a moment's indecisiveness. He knew the fight was over for now, but at the same time recognized that, as long as the lynx was near, there was a good chance of her taking over the den again. Furthermore, he remembered the ambush from above. It would not be comfortable to have such a capable enemy in the immediate area.

He followed his nose easily as far as the game trail, then lost her scent completely in the jumble of old deer smells. He had just about decided she was on her way back to the den when he heard the sharp, ringing babble of a frightened squirrel. He whirled and headed toward the lake, taking the precaution of moving off the trail into the middle branches of the evergreens. Suddenly he stopped, excitement quickening at the sight of the dappled silver shape crouched in the next tree and thirty feet below.

Slowly, the fisher worked to a lower level. He eased out on a huge, downsweeping bough that reached within easy leaping distance of the branch directly above the lynx's head. He gathered his strength beneath him, and with a blood-curdling shriek, shot down the curve of the limb and launched out across the gap.

The lynx felt the jar as the fisher hit the branch beside her, and she tumbled from her perch. She managed to twist and land running, heading full tilt to the west, but she had little chance of escaping the fisher in the heavy woods. Though she used trees for ambushes and escapes, when she ran it was on the ground, around bushes and over fallen timber. The fisher, traveling with startling speed through the trees, was up to her in a matter of seconds. She swerved eastward, trying to reach the open ground around the bay. Within seconds, she heard his claws and saw the dark gleam of his fur above her. Once again she tried to cut west, hoping she might lose him in the marshes, but he refused to let her move in any direction but due north, unswervingly away from the den. He was quite unaware that he was forcing her into a trap, driving her toward the promontory where the old man's hardwoods grew, but the lynx knew the area much better than he and fathomed fully what was happening.

The fisher and the lynx faced each other for the last time that day on a fragile bough over the glassy water. The lynx worked her way out to the quivering tip. The fisher crept toward her in his slow, ominous stalk. Balancing precariously, the lynx took a final swat at her tormentor. She felt the bough beneath her shudder and begin to crack. The fisher backed to the thicker, safer portion of the branch and watched as she leaped into the water.

The lynx hit in a brief-lived shower of droplets. She made no attempt to come ashore, but swam strongly toward the far side of the marsh. North of her, on the open body of the lake, a flock of migrating Canada geese stopped, craning their black-stocking necks cautiously forward until she passed. Then slowly, weighed down by the fatigue of a long night's flying, they paddled in stolid, interlacing vees of ripples toward the rice.

In the spruce, the fisher yawned and stretched, blinking as the blazing edge of the sun cleared the horizon. Finally he left the tree and trotted toward his den. He was luxuriously tired, but he took the time to groom himself before flipping his tail across his nose and dropping off to sleep.

Fifteen minutes later he was awake again, his ears cocked toward a sound he had never heard before. It was a melody, high-pitched and wonderfully sweet, which wavered upward until it reached a single unbelievbly pure note. Curious, he eased out on the ledge.

Almost exactly below him a tiny deer mouse sat, balanced on a fallen branch, oblivious to the world around him. The light struck rubies from his eyes and glowed through his translucent ears as he lifted his whiskered muzzle high to sing a morning hymn to the rising of the sun.

7

THAT YEAR, the autumn died beautifully, with a shiver of quaking aspens and a gentle rain of perfect days that flowed like warm tears down the face of the north. To the fisher, they were days and nights of magic, a time of discovery, when he experienced a swelling sense of belonging as he ranged the lake, laying out the boundaries of his personal hunting preserve.

The tract was in the shape of a great, equilateral triangle—two miles to a side—of second-growth timber. The fisher haunted the great triangle every night for a week after his battle with the lynx. Hunting was easier than he had ever known, for the dense ground cover was the home for literally thousands of rabbits, weasels, mice, and voles. The trees swarmed with squirrels; birds there were in plenty, grouse and jays, owls and tender, toothsome wrens. Along one edge of the triangle, the marsh offered a fantastic harvest of frogs and shore birds—and, he discovered quite by chance, muskrats.

He found out about the muskrats when he saw a fox working through the belly-high water toward a cone of mud and rushes. He watched the slow, purposeful approach, the sudden, swift attack, and the fox's pleased gallop back to shore with a squirming muskrat gripped tightly in his jaws. The fisher tried the same trick and, on the third attempt, managed to reach a muskrat before the muskrat reached his plunge hole.

He followed and spied on many animals in the triangle, unconsciously filling in the gaps in his education left by his mother's death. From the weasels he learned the use of cover, from the foxes the way to circle a rabbit until it ran itself out; the deer showed him how to blend motionlessly with any background, and the squirrels and jays taught him the meaning of their danger calls. The bears educated him in berries and skunks.

The fisher met his first bear family one clear evening near the marsh. A chorus of childlike wails drew him to the western edge, where he found an old sow going after her two half-grown cubs for having dared climb a cedar. A few powerful blows against the trunk brought the youngsters sliding down; a wallop to the ears drove home the lesson that cedars were unsafe as a refuge, that the corky bark simply would not hold a cub's claws firmly enough.

Both cubs were still whimpering when their mother grunted and led them off to a clump of thorny gooseberry bushes. There, the cubs trotted eagerly to separate bushes. Above in the trees, the fisher watched as each cub sat unright before his personal bush and, unmindful of the thorns, drew it forward to strip it of leaves and berries. Then each settled on his haunches, lifted an arm, inspected it critically, and licked it clean of the succulent fruit. For an hour the cubs labored until, with stomachs bulging pleasantly, they exploded into rollicking play. The old sow watched tolerantly, then with a quiet, whimpering call, dropped to all fours. The cubs broke apart instantly and followed. The fisher, intensely curious, padded over to the bushes the moment they were out of sight.

The ends of the branches were bare, but farther in, there were a few purple globules. He sniffed one, wrinkled back his lips, and nipped it free. He blinked, his eyes warming at the honeyed flavor, then began carefully to pick the berries out of their thorny nests. By the time he finished the moon was down. He belched and trotted home, staggering slightly from the jab of a belly ache.

He came across the family again two days after the berry session. A sharp scraping and hammering from the spruces before his den drew him out early in the afternoon. The bears were on a grub hunt. The fisher saw the old sow hook her short, sharp claws into a rotting log, heave it over and split it open with three smashing blows. The cubs scampered forward to lick up the slow-moving grubs. The old sow nosed a patch of sandy loam and called her cubs to her side. They watched alertly as their mother placed a paw flat on the ochre patch, then lifted and licked it. Tentatively at first, then eagerly, they followed suit.

When they left, the fisher examined the spot. A thin trickle of ants was struggling through the hills and valleys of the paw prints. The fisher extended a foot as the bears had done. He jerked it back as the ants swarmed into his fur, then licked experimentally. He savored the ants for a moment, decided he really did not like the sour, pickled taste, and shook the rest from his fur. Then he tried one of the slimy, dun-colored slugs inching along the wood. It was even more offensive. He spat it out, feeling very much betrayed.

His final disillusionment came that evening. He had slept an hour later than usual, and when he padded down from the ridge, he found the bears at the foot, foraging among the berry bushes. They were strung out in a line, and when the fisher saw he was between the mother and the larger of the cubs, he pulled back into the shadows. He knew intuitively that it was unwise to come between a mother and her young at any time.

A flicker of black and white caught his attention, and he crouched low, watching while a placid, old male skunk sauntered into the berry patch. The fisher knew there were several skunks in the triangle of timber. He had seen the den where two females lived with their combined families of seven young. But it was the first time the fisher had seen this particular solitary male, even though the old bachelor had built his burrow only a hundred yards away from the females, so that in March he would never have too far to plod through the snow before he found a mate.

Actually, the fisher's knowledge of skunks was limited. His mother had always left them severely alone. He looked on with mounting curiosity to see how the bears would deal with the animal. The skunk sniffed the fragile breeze, gave the bears an offhand look, and plodded calmly toward a skunk currant, twenty-five feet upwind of the crouching fisher. He settled back in his haunches, then reached up and nipped one of the bristly, red fruits. He chewed it reflectively, dropped to all fours, ambled downwind, and began to sample the fleshy, red chokeberries.

It was then that the larger cub saw him. Obviously, he knew nothing of skunks and he was fooled by the half-sitting, half-standing posture of the skunk into believing he was face to face with a particularly large specimen of the greatest of all bear delicacies, the squirrel. With an eager cough, the cub rumbled forward. The skunk growled as he swung to face the bear, his eyeshine a bright, flashing amber. The old sow saw the movement and turned. Her dim eyesight could make nothing of the form of the skunk at first. Then she spotted the telltale vee of white, and barked out the low, double woof of her danger signal. The smaller cub joined her instantly. The larger skidded to stop and looked back questioningly.

The skunk seemed quite unafraid of the cub. He lifted his tail straight in the air, but as yet the white-flecked tip was left drooping. The cub leaned forward to sniff the air. The skunk began to grow angry. From where he lay, the fisher heard him go through a remarkably broad repertoire of grunts, mumbles and grinding of teeth, ending in a swift tattoo of short-tempered foot stamping. The cub took an experimental step. The skunk whirled, his lifted tail facing the cub. The old sow repeated her urgent danger call, the cub froze, and the skunk flipped up the tip of his tail and fired.

The cub screamed as the oily, yellow spray bit into

his eyes, sending tears down his snout. His mother started to lunge forward, but hesitated as the skunk swung his upraised tail toward her. With a final snort for the whining cub, the skunk cocked his tail and stumped away. The sow immediately lumbered toward her cub, but stopped in disgust as she caught the full blast of him. She coughed a warning to stay away as she backed to her other cub and led it into the forest. The large cub, wailing piteously and still nearly blind, staggered after them. She let him follow, but coughed a warning every time he came closer than twenty feet.

The fisher had been far enough from the skunk to miss the worst of the blast, but the night breeze had lifted a thin cloud of the vapor. The stench was appalling, and the moment the clearing was empty, he raced away, not knowing or caring where he went. It was then that he discovered he was carrying the stench with him. He tried to outrun it, but each time he stopped, the breeze lifted the stink from his flank. Gradually, he found he could just stand himself if he either stayed on the move or kept his rear end downwind of his front.

Hunting was out of the question, and he certainly had no intention of taking this awful smell into his clean and comfortable den. So, he went to the top of the sentinel spruce, carefully selecting a branch that faced the night breeze. He took a gagging dab at his flank. The smell immediately clogged his nose. He leaned his head over the branch and vomited. He took another lick, and another, preferring the retching to leaving his coat smelling as it did. Bit by bit through the long night, with the nausea roiling inside him, he cleaned the fouled fur. Morning found him still in the tree, wracked by vomiting, but at least able to bear himself. That night he hunted and, surprisingly, managed to keep down most of what he ate. But it was three days before he allowed himself to return to his den, and for weeks after, whenever his coat was wet, a very real reminder of the skunk was with him.

8

As THE DAYS PASSED, the young fisher, who had missed spring through the cloistered months of infancy and known only summer for the rest of his short life, found autumn a time of bewildering change. For while the aspens and the birches bowed to weep a flood of crisping leaves upon the ground, while the wild rice and burr reeds browned to a frost-burned autumn frailty, and all around the land was sighing with ebbing vegetable energy, the animals and birds were infected with a vibrant surging in the blood.

By day and by night the birds gathered, flocking to the mounting call of distance. Singly or in a fluttering rabble they fled southward, the flycatchers to Central America, the purple martins to Brazil, and the regimented flocks of Canada geese down the great Mississippi flyway toward the hunters' waiting guns. Those that stayed—the gray jays and nuthatches and the black and brown-capped chickadees—were barely aware that the others had left. They were too busy gorging to rebuild a protective layer of comfortable fat after the summer strain of nesting.

The bears ate all day and all night, stuffing until the layers of fat were a solid three inches thick. The chipmunks built huge hoards of nuts and seeds, and then constructed sleeping quarters on top of the storehouses, so that, come the winter, they might never need to leave their nests. The squirrels harvested mushrooms by the thousands, cramming the spongy caps into the crotches of the trees to dry in the sun and wind. Even the little creatures of the forest floor felt the drive as they raced with frenetic energy through the tunnels beneath the grass, dodging the ever-watching owls. And all across the north, in the sweet, moss-scented clearings, the moose battled bravely in the twilight.

Deep within himself, the fisher felt the same October intensity, and so he plunged into a compulsive round of explorations that opened up his hunting range with remarkable speed. Sleep became secondary. Each dawn he came to his den to doze a few hours away, but by noon he was back on the trail again. He hurried under the inner pressure guiding all northern animals through the last, short weeks before the awful stress of a subarctic winter, answering the intuitive drive to prepare for the months when the environment itself becomes the most implacable of enemies. He moved with such purpose that, within three days, he had quartered the entire western shore of the lake.

More and more, as the month advanced, the fisher saw the tides of change sweep across the forest. Gradually, the nightly insect symphony faded into silence, as the crickets, stuporous with cold, only occasionally found the will to shudder their torpid wing cases together in a forlorn and lonely chirrup. In the bushes, the fireflies flickered and went out. The bats went next.

Gathering at dusk, the colonies of little brown myotis searched the air, and finding the insects nearly gone, dipped over the lake for a final, flying sip of the cool water and fled south. The silver-haired and red bats followed singly, while high above, the frosted mahogany shapes of the hoary bats shuttled a last, weaving pattern against the banks of moon-washed clouds before they too turned their backs to the solitary pole star. Only the big brown bats remained, drowsily searching for a last few beetles before retiring to hollow trees, where they would hang head downward in a sleep beyond sleep, waiting for the spring.

The bears now moved slowly through the thickets, stretching and yawning themselves awake in the afternoon sun, ambling in an aimless way while their eyes continually sought the fallen log or hollow beneath a tall tree's roots where the lengthening shadows told them they could sleep in peace. The skunks laid claim to winter burrows beneath wood or rockfalls, the females and their kits together, the old males solitary and alone. The tiny meadow and woodland jumping mice, their tails half again as long as their bodies, mined winter burrows three feet deep beneath the forest floor. Muskrats shuffled resolutely overland, leaving their houses in the marsh to dig new homes in the banks of the streams. And some left the streams to build their domes in the marsh. Beneath the densest thickets, the snowshoe rabbits sat motionless, while the mysterious alchemy of the north slowly changed their summer coats to a protective winter white.

In the dense stand of pine and tamarack and balsam

poplar north of the lake, the flying squirrels grew suddenly delirious. All the warm nights of summer, they had practiced their skills between the leaf-dark limbs. But now, the leaves were slipping to the ground, opening hundreds of new flyways. Where before had been screens of foliage to maneuver through and past to the uncertain safety of the half-seen trunk, there now stretched bare branches, with no retreat where a lurking killer might hide. For the youngest squirrels it was a time of magic. Even elders joined the play, for this was the season when, with nests repaired and lined with freshly shredded bark and lichen, with winter food gathered and all but the youngest capable of caring for themselves, the entire colony could lose itself in an orgy of flight. The moment the sun touched the western rim, the squirrels came out. First the older males, watchful and alert beneath their exuberance; then the young and yearlings, irrepressibly excited; finally the females, cautious but exhilarated. Boisterously they burst toward the heights to fly together in the dying light.

Inevitably, the joy was crossed by death. Perhaps once, at most two or three times an evening, the light would flicker from the talons of a great horned owl or flash from the yellow catlike eyes of a great gray owl. On utterly silent wings the birds would glide between the branches, and a single, agonized shriek would transfix the luminous air, bursting bright blisters of fear in the hearts of the little fliers. Yet, within the half-hour, the high, open crowns of the trees would be dotted with the metronoming shapes again.

The fisher found the hunting both excellent and

exciting in this pale patch of softwood timber, at first among the squirrels, but later among those that preyed on them. Especially on the pine martens, for when he learned that each marten weighed as much as three to five squirrels, he decided it was foolish to strain through chase after chase when, if he waited, he could accomplish just as much in one attack. He felt no conceit in having chased down a hunter swifter even than the swiftest squirrel. He only felt exhilarated by the chase and filled with the simple pleasure of having accomplished what he had set himself to do.

He laid out his hunting range a full three miles north of the lake. It was a landscape immensely rich in trees; pines grew in abundance, even a few majestic white pines, as straight and proud as the masts of the sailing ships they once had supplied; jack pines too, holding their humpbacked cones above the harsher soil. Tamaracks, stripped of their bright, green halos of summer needles, sprang stark and straight from the moist hollows; through them, black and white spruces lifted slender spires of blue-green above the modest, downward sweep of their lower boughs.

The whitetail deer were coming into rut. All summer the deer had been apart, driven into the densest thickets by clouds of insects. The rippling glow of their butterscotch-brown coats had faded under the onslaught of mosquitoes and deer flies. By late summer, bucks and does alike were patched and shaggy. Then, the first frost had wiped the air clear, and the deer had plunged into a marathon round of heavy feeding. Hair by hair, the rusty, careworn coats had gone. In their place had come the magnificent, heavy, dove-gray winter dress. Bellies and muscles had filled out. The bucks had shadow-boxed the thickets until the layers of velvet were stripped from their antlers, revealing crowns of proud tines, hard and polished and regal.

Now, nervous and tensed under the press of instinct, each buck slipped between the trees like a wraith, seeking the doe that would give his urge for battle meaning. And because he was an animal and, at most, an ingenuous and rather simple being, each battle fought became the most magnificent and courageous, and every doe won the most desirable of creatures to meet and mount and herd with through the months ahead. The does, of course, had no illusions. They knew perfectly well what it was all about and always turned to the victor, no matter how coyly they had encouraged the vanquished.

The fisher was watching two bucks battle near the northern boundary of his preserve when he first discovered that somewhere near was another of his kind. Crouched low in a spruce, he was suddenly aware of two flecks of cold, yellow-green light turned unwaveringly his way from the trees rimming the far side of the clearing. He knew it for the eyeshine of another watcher, but could see no detail—only a shapeless, black form, a dark center in a charcoal shadow, with two pinpoints of icy flame floating neatly at the heart. Marking the position mentally, he dropped from his perch and slipped around the clearing. But, though he moved slowly and with immense care, when he reached the tree, the watcher was gone. He climbed gingerly into the boughs and snuffled through the well of shadow where the creature had lain. The hair on the nape of his neck literally lifted, for through the skunky spruce he caught the scent of another fisher. It was unmistakably a fisher's smell, like his own, yet tantalizingly different, with a distinctive, rich musk that brought a fleeting image of his dead mother. He turned to trail the other, then stopped, suddenly aware that he wanted no company until he was fully established in his own territory. So, with a final sniff, he dropped to the ground and turned south.

By the middle of the third week, he was plumbing the mysteries of the heavily forested region northeast of the lake. There were four fox dens dotted around this side of the lake, a main nurse lair, and three small safety dens where pups could be hidden from danger. All had been dug by a fine, red male and his mate, a big vixen with a superb, silver-tipped black coat. They had raised a mixed bag of young red, cross, and black, but now, as the autumnal frosts thickened their coats, the ties that had made them a family were fading away. When the fisher had first entered the stand, the seven had been hunting together. In less than a week, four had gone, answering the strange inward call that would send each wandering alone to seek and find a mid-winter mate and recreate the pattern for another year.

Fifty yards to the south of the main fox lair, the fisher discovered a porcupine colony. To his surprise, there were not one, but ten porcupines humping like big, bristly, black burrs beneath and among the boughs of the star-hung trees. They paid scant attention to the fisher, even when he stood in full view. Two of the larger males glared toward him, but when he settled on his haunches, they turned their backs and went about their business.

Their business was breeding. After a summer of happy solitude, they had come from miles around to fulfill their seasonal debt to their kind. They had behaved much as they did when meeting through the year, playfully and with joy in each other's company. The big males had indulged in giddy sparring contests, sitting on their barbed haunches and trying to shove their opponents off balance, but always taking care to stay clear of the spearing quills. One young male had found a fallen branch, hollowed by the mandibles of ground beetles and carpenter ants, and it was his pleasure to sit beside it every night, drumming with his forefeet and listening to the resonant notes he produced. The females had lain on their backs, juggling sticks with their four stubby legs, or had stood upright on their hind feet and danced, heads cocked to the side and eyes half closed, listening to some internal rhythm. Occasionally, the males had joined them, shifting from one foot to the other in a matching, primitive two-step. Or the males had sparred with them, or followed in ungainly, romping chases through the trees.

But slowly, under the spell of the lengthening nights, a distinct feeling of tension had begun to grow in the colony. The males, ever sensitive to the females' emotional temperature, had drawn back. They had played among themselves, but fitfully and without the earlier absorption. The females had stumped edgily through the forest, rubbing against the trunks, climbing trees, and immediately coming down again, gnawing the sticks they hitherto had juggled, and whining nervously beneath their growing hunger. The males had followed at a distance, waiting, carefully inspecting the patches of ground where the females had deposited their scent and lifting the earth in cupped forepaws to sniff it.

The fisher came upon them as they were playing out the last act in the yearly drama. The females were quiet now, sitting close to the males, and waiting for the internal clock to tell them their fertile time had come, that the twelve-hour period out of the entire year when they could successfully conceive had begun. As the fisher watched, he saw a big female turn and sniff the male beside her suggestively. He swung around and touched his nose to hers. They shuffled back from each other and rose on their hind legs. With a gentle swaying of their heads, they stepped forward and embraced, their noses touching once again. This was the trigger. Instantly, the female was on all fours, her quills laid flat and her tail turned up along her back, presenting a softly furred cushion to the male. With a clatter of quills, he mounted, not gripping her in any way, but leaving her to decide when the embrace was through. It lasted a scant five minutes. The female slid out from beneath him, and approached another male. Twice more she repeated the courtship pattern, until she was finally satisfied. Then she clambered into a birch, and began happily to stuff herself with the sweet underbark.

All night the fisher watched. He had no knowledge of the forces at work in the colony, but so strong was the undercurrent of tension that he grasped intuitively that an event of major importance was taking place. And so he did not kill, he only watched.

9

THE FISHER had been to the old Ojibway's cabin twice since leaving, the night after his battle with the lynx, and again a week later. Each time the cabin had been quiet, the air free of the smell of woodsmoke. The smaller of the old man's canoes had been lifted from the water. The larger had disappeared from the small, floating pier. The first time the fisher came, the cabin had seemed merely empty. The second, there had been an air of loneliness and desertion about the place. Now the clearing almost shouted of the old man's return.

The fisher padded swiftly up to the cabin door and sniffed at the jamb. The cabin was very quiet. Impulsively, he slipped around to the side. He rustled through the crisp bracken that all summer had made a bright green footrest for the chimney and trotted over to the chicken run. The birds were alert behind the screening. The old rooster saw the fisher's slender shape and dived back into the guano-smelling darkness with a squawk. His fear communicated to the hens, and for a moment their babbling burst through the clearing. The fisher moved on, and the air was still again.

He inspected the thick, fragrant piles of fresh wood chips and sawdust around a huge, black spruce stump the old man used for a chopping block, then moved past the ramped piles of cordwood stacked against the cabin and on down to the pier and the canoe. Above the damp varnish smell was the scent of the man, an odor that repelled him and yet hinted at an underlying kinship that he found as disturbing as it was appealing. He snorted to clear his nostrils and moved to the bow where the man smell was much less intense. A faint creak from the direction of the cabin sent him gliding up the shore.

The old Ojibway stood in the doorway, dressed in a suit of bright red, thermal underwear. He was happy to see the fisher, even though the animal was obviously behind the ruckus in the henhouse that had wakened him. For a moment he thought of the screening across the top of the run. It was rusted near the roof line, and he pondered whether to string it out another year. Then he shrugged. If the fisher decided to raid his chickens, there was little he could do short of killing the animal, and he had no intention of that.

The Ojibway had been home for three days, and it had been with a great feeling of relief that he had paddled his heavy canoe down the lake. This year as always, he had been startled by the changes wrought during his short absence. The lake had held a muted hush, for the summer birds had fled. Even the loons had sculled southeastward, to spend the winter rocking among the eternal waves, far out on the breast of the Atlantic. The butterfly-bright trees facing his cabin had shed their particolored leaves. And the butterflies themselves had gone, the commas and the mourning cloaks into hibernation, the monarchs on their dangerous trip to Mexico.

The old man walked down to the shore and cupped the cool water to his face. After breakfast, he set about his own lumbering—cutting, splitting, and stacking his winter supply of wood. By mid-morning he was stripped to the waist, with the sun casting burnished highlights from his sweat-streaked skin. A family of chipmunks scampered out of the woods, climbed his woodpile, and lay basking in the mellow sunlight. An old, gray jay winged across the stream and banked into the spruces behind the cabin. He stared down at the Indian, like a huge, overgrown black-capped chickadee, and murmured his low, hopeful, sighing call.

The old man walked into the cabin, reappearing with a strip of dried deer meat. He cut a piece and tossed it beneath the spruce, imitating the jay's blurred call. The big bird dropped earthward with a rattling chuckle, and watching the man with a bright and tolerant eye, began to pull the meat apart with his stubby bill. The old Indian cut the rest into slender strips, walked to the woodpile, and coaxed the chipmunks forward to eat from his hands. When he returned to work, he left them perched in a row like little old men, each nibbling a strip of meat that dangled between his paws.

The rest of the morning was spent working on a new pair of snowshoes. He chose the classic Ojibway pattern, a large rounded diamond nearly two feet wide and four long, the pattern his people had used for over a thousand years. By early afternoon the work was ready for steaming, but he set it aside, took a willow and rush basket, and set out across the bay in the small canoe. He cut through the spruces to the boggy edge of the marsh, where the mountain cranberries grew in scarlet profusion. He half filled the basket, then spent an hour digging through the soggy ground beneath the tamaracks, selecting the sinewy, thread-like rootlets to use as stitching for the seams of birchbark containers and for seizing and repairing the bindings of his narrow willow-wand fish trap. Finally, he took his harvest back to the canoe. Then, impulsively, he turned and walked along the old deer trail to the ridge.

It was his first visit to the ridge since his return, and he looked over his lake with pleasure. A timid breeze was puffing experimentally from the north, wiping the air almost clean of insects. A torpid wasp blundered past the old man's legs, searching drowsily for an even more torpid spider. He watched it for a moment, then saw the regular rows of claw marks scratched into the hard rind of the roots leading over the edge of the ridge. He plucked a small tuft of fur free from a snag in the roots and fingered the dark, silky strands. He knew it to be fisher fur at once. Swiftly, he slipped off his moccasins and began to work down the root ladder.

The fisher awoke with a start as the Indian's feet sent a rattle of crumbling shards down the cliff face. Poised and wary, he edged out just as the old man reached a solid footing. The animal knew that a simple, swift attack would tumble the Indian off the ledge, just as it had tumbled the lynx. Yet, he did not really wish to attack. And his unwillingness disturbed him as much as his not understanding the reason for it. It was not from gratitude, for gratitude was an emotion foreign to him. Besides, what the old man had done for him was in the past and gone. The present fact was that the Indian stood vulnerably before him, and disturbingly close to the den. Yet, the surging anger of attack would not come. Quite simply, he knew the old man would not harm him, that in a world of enemies, actual and potential, the Ojibway offered no threat. With that knowledge, the fisher satisfied himself with a snarl of gentle warning. The old man smiled, turned, and climbed from sight.

The fisher listened while the Indian scuffed his feet into his moccasins and walked with whispering strides down the slope. He smoothed the fur on his chest, scratched his ear, then slipped up on the ridge and followed the man. He caught up just as the Indian started across the shelving rocks to the bay. Watching from inside the screen of branches, the fisher saw him stiffen, raise his hand to shield his eyes, and stare intently to the north. The Indian tensed visibly, walked quickly to the water's edge, cast off in his canoe, and stroked across the bay toward his cabin.

After a moment, the fisher saw what the old man had seen, the dark sliver of a canoe with a single occupant paddling southward. Intrigued, he made for the stream and the Ojibway's clearing. Within ten minutes, he was settled in and watching, his vantage point a small spruce whose open-grown branches clothed the trunk nearly to the ground.

The Ojibway stood at the pier, waited until the stranger in the canoe hailed him, then lifted his hand in welcome. The canoe bumped against the floating platform. The old man picked up the painter and fastened it with a quick bowline to the mooring stake.

The newcomer heaved himself out of the canoe, shook the Indian's hand, then stretched with arms akimbo, and kneaded the muscles in the small of his back. He was easily a head shorter and considerably broader than the old man. Against the Indian's lithe slimness, he presented a picture of short, compacted power. Everything about him was hairy, from the beard and the unruly mop of black that curled around his neck to the mass of fur springing from his chest above the vee of his unbuttoned shirt, and on down to the hazy, dark patches smudging the backs of his hands.

The breeze brought the mixed scents of the two to the fisher, and he could easily separate the Indian's mellow smell from the rancid sweatiness of the other. He bristled unconsciously, angry at the memories the scent evoked of another lovely, sunlit afternoon. He cocked his ears as the stranger's laugh floated to him, a short, full-throated bark with an underlying rasp.

The bearded man heaved a bulging packsack from the canoe. A loose bundle of bright objects was caught in the straps. They flashed in the sun and clinked metallically as the stranger bent to free them. He did not see the Indian go suddenly rigid at the sound. But he looked up curiously when the old man spoke, surprised at the swift change of tone. The Indian said some quiet, quick words, and the stranger answered with an offhand laugh. He straightened, his fists on his hips.

The fisher had no knowledge of what was happening, but he was intensely aware of the surge of emotion flaring between the men. The argument was brief. After the first, swift interchange, the old man's voice became soft and decisive. The stranger's voice was a harsh contrast, though he neither raised it, nor let it shift from the original coldness. Finally, the Indian gestured emphatically to the stream, then up to the ridge and along the line of trees north of his cabin. The stranger shot a single, terse question. The Ojibway did not speak his answer. Instead, he slowly lifted his arm and pointed due west across the lake. The bearded man grunted, tossed his packsack back into the bow, and kicked off from the shore.

For a long time the old Ojibway stared after the canoe. The beauty of the westering sun washed away his anger, so that by the time the man was half across the lake, he was calm again. But the weight of his distress had not left him, nor the memory of the apprehension that had stabbed his heart at the first clink of the traps. As he walked toward his cabin, his mind was haunted by the images of fear and pain and death he knew must inevitably follow in the bearded stranger's footsteps.

The old man's practiced eye caught a flicker of silver near the trunk of the tree closest to his cabin. When he saw the fisher staring down, he frowned, for the animal with his damaged coat brought a personal twist to his fears. Like all the animals around the lake, the fisher knew nothing of traps. If he were caught, the trapper would take one look at the white flash of the burn scar and not even bother to take the pelt for curing. He would simply kill the fisher and leave his body to the scavengers.

At least, the Indian thought with a sigh, the man was late in starting. Still, there were many months to go before the season's end in April, and many animals would die. He prayed the fisher would not be one of them. The old man could only hope curiosity would keep him to this side of the lake, for he had told the trapper he held all the land between the ridge and the northernmost stream under a crown land grant. It was an outright lie, but surprisingly the trapper had believed him. With luck, he would keep believing, and the animals this side of the lake would be spared. There was, unfortunately, nothing more the old man could do.

The fisher was very much on edge, disturbed by what he had witnessed. He began to pick his way down through the branches and paused halfway. The old man had gone to the chicken run and was now coming back. The fisher waited as the man rustled through the bracken stubble, laid a single, buff-colored egg at the foot of the tree, then strode across to the cabin. Cautiously, the fisher slipped to the ground and nosed the egg. It was still warm, with the fresh scent of the hen clinging to it. Delicately, he rolled it around to the far side of the trunk, propped it between his paws, and nipped off the top. He lapped out the contents. His equanimity restored, he batted the empty shell playfully, stretched with a satisfying ripple of muscle, and trotted across the open ground. He made no effort at concealment, but passed directly in front of the door, gazing quizzically at where the old man stood. The Indian raised his hand in a timeworm gesture of greeting, but his eyes held a look of deep concern as he watched the fisher fade beneath the screen of trees.

10

IT WAS FULL DARK by the time the fisher ambled across the mud-packed rim of the beaver dam. Overhead, the quartering moon trailed behind it the sparkled dust webs of the Milky Way. The night surged with movement and tiny night sounds, but the fisher paid them no heed, for he was drawn farther west toward the spring-fed pond, where a hint of light gleamed persuasively through the trees. He knew the area well, for the pond was one of the apexes of the great triangle of second-growth timber. To the north, across the still, black surface, a dense wall of spruces crept down to within a yard of the water's edge. Their strangulated boughs framed the sagging roof and mossy walls of a trapper's ancient cabin, whose canted doorway peered across the pond like a huge, sorrowing eye.

A small, orange campfire flickered on the northern shore. The fisher picked his way through a tangled mat of spikemoss, scouring rush, and bristly clubmoss, and up into the trees crowding the old cabin. The trapper sat before its door with the fire ruddy on his face, framed by a lean-to of rough-hacked boughs. He gripped a battered briar in his teeth, and the bland tobacco smoke drifted to the fisher, mixed with the harsher smells of woodsmoke, bacon fat, and the all-pervading stink of sweat. In the blackness behind the man, the fisher could see the faint eyeshine of other watchers, the orange glint of rabbit, the icy green of weasel, and farther back, the green-gold blink of a fox and the softer, amber tint of a deer. Slowly, he moved toward the fire, unaware that his own cold, green eyeshine pinpointed him just as clearly.

The man was adjusting his traps, carefully touching up the catch mechanisms. The fisher cocked his ears to the soft screech of the file. He was strangely attracted by the gleam of flames on the bright metal and by the delicate movements of the trapper's fingers. He flinched slightly as above, a saw-whet owl threw a tremulous whinny into the night. The trapper's eyes narrowed as they searched the black wall beyond the firelight. He stiffened as his gaze swept across, then fastened on the darkness where the fisher lay. Very slowly, his hand moved to the rifle propped against his packsacks. The fisher watched curiously while he slid it across his lap, worked the bolt back, and with a snick of oiled metal, levered a round into the barrel. Then, in one smooth, practiced movement, he snugged the butt against his shoulder and swung the muzzle toward the shadows.

The fisher tensed when the trapper lifted the rifle, recognizing its danger, but not perceiving how the danger could strike across such a distance. He watched the barrel foreshorten until it became a small circle of blued metal, pierced by a tiny, bottomless hole. He crouched, hypnotized, while flickers of apprehension chased through him, then swerved to spring. As he did, the trapper fired.

He barely heard the explosion of the rifle. It was lost in the shattering impact of the bullet. He felt his hindquarters go out from under him, and suddenly he was half off the swaying branch, scrabbling frantically at the rough, flaky bark. He had no sensation in his hind legs. From his hips down, they felt completely dead and lifeless. A dark glisten of blood streaked his left flank from the hip to the knee. He saw the trapper ram another shell home, then come slowly to his feet. The fisher clenched his teeth tightly and struggled to force movement into his hind legs. His right leg began to lift slowly. Concentrating intensely, he swung it forward. He worked entirely by sight, for even as it moved, the leg felt as numb and disembodied as the battered one hanging limply by its side.

With an immense surge of effort, the fisher heaved his hindquarters up on the broad limb, and dragged himself awkwardly to a small, shielded pocket of interlaced branches. The trapper cast about the undergrowth, then stared upward. He poked the muzzle of the rifle into the dense mats of needles. The fisher lay motionless, three feet above his head, not stirring as the rifle grazed his numbed thigh. After a final searching glance, the trapper walked back to the fire. He clicked the safety catch on the rifle and laid it against the packs. Then he stretched on the ground, rolled himself in his blanket, and closed his eyes.

The fisher remained unmoving in the tree. Slowly, sensation began to creep back into his right leg, and he winced as the cold, intense burning spread from his spine down to his toes. His left leg was still numb, though he could feel the first hint of burning starting in the upper thigh. He nosed his flank, snuffling at the taste of his own blood, trying to discover the extent of the damage. His tongue could only discover one area of broken skin, high on the flank, a small, neat gouge directly over the crest of his pelvis. In passing, the bullet had scooped a shallow runnel through the thin layer of flesh and muscle, lightly brushing the bone. The shock, transmitted to the spinal cord, had left his legs temporarily paralyzed. Slowly now, the nerves were regaining function, sending movement down, carrying pain up.

The trapper stirred and reached out a hand to push a length of wood farther into the low flames. The fisher stayed perfectly still until the breathing changed to a muted snore, then eased himself cautiously along the branch. His left leg still hung uselessly, and the right hurt incredibly whenever he put his full weight on it. But he levered himself onto the trunk, and slowly backed down. He fell the last three feet, thudding into a crumbling patch of shriveled goldthread. His left leg twisted under him as he hit, and he burst out with a high, muffled shriek. He heard the trapper stir. He pressed tightly to the ground, quivering until the man's breathing regained its deep and rhythmical note. He hunched his back, and heaved himself to his feet. Abruptly, he realized his left hip was in action once again. When he moved it slowly and experimentally, the lances of pain darted like sharp razors toward the still numbed paw—but it moved.

For three days the fisher stayed close to his den and during those days, winter struck. It struck hard and fast, as if to kill the autumn with one fierce blow. The temperature fell twenty degrees in one night, then slumped a further ten at dawn.

For the first day and a half the fisher slept fitfully, prodded intermittently awake by recurring spasms of pain. By the second day, he was able to scramble to the ridge to relieve himself. But the dull ache in his hindquarters warned him against trying to hunt. At the end of forty-eight hours, he was still able to forget his hunger in sullen, dark anger at the thought of man. It was a tangible thing now, overriding the fact that one of the men he had known had been trustworthy. No longer did he see the three as separate individuals. Now they were all part of a single entity—man—and in his mind he felt only enmity.

His temper was not improved by his discomfort, for added to the pain was the cold, and as the one faded, the other grew. Finally, he was forced to start moving around the small den to restore circulation. He discovered that with movement came an easing of the tension and aching in his thighs. By the evening of the third day most of his strength had returned. His hip was extremely tender, but beyond this and a faint weakness in his thighs, the only permanent reminder was a lack of sensation in two toes of his left foot. And that was nothing compared to the hunger in his belly, for like the mink and weasels, his metabolism worked at such a pace that he could not go too long without food. Five days at most.

The sky was clearing as he climbed up to the ridge. In the old black spruce a monstrous great-horned owl ruffled the white feathers of his throat collar and sent out a resonant, deep, triple hoot. To the northeast, a fox barked, waited, then barked again. But there was no answer, and the night closed around the lonely sound.

The fisher shivered as the raw wind crept beneath his coat. He came down from the ridge at a fast trot, and set out to hunt immediately, slipping swiftly through the trees, willing to take anything that moved. Somewhere in his brain was the instinctive knowledge that only food would bring the warmth he craved and stop his body drawing on its few reserves.

He stalked and killed a scurrying deer mouse, but the ounce of meat and bone scarcely took the edge off the gnawing in his stomach. Twice he flushed rabbits, but lost them each time when his thigh muscles gave out after a short chase. Angrily, he cut over to the marsh, hoping to dig a muskrat out of its house. To his surprise, he found the boggy edge stiff with ice, and the still water covered by a flexible black skin barely strong enough to take his weight. Gingerly, then with increasing confidence, he walked out on the rubbery surface. A mud and rush cone was only fifteen feet away. The faint warmth and pungent smell told him a muskrat crouched inside. He poised himself, then with a sudden burst of energy, struck at the structure. His claws merely glanced off. He tried again, and once more, but cold had set the soggy mass of rush and mud as hard as concrete. His claws only left shallow, star-edged furrows down the glittering cone.

He tried two more cones, attacking with a growing fury that left him panting and snarling. Finally, with his feet aching from the bite of the ice he gave up and moved back to the shore. The wind began to pick up. It ruffled his coat, prodding beneath the dense fur. He swung about and faded beneath the trees, his mind suddenly illuminated by the memory of the porcupines near the northeastern shore.

The mouth of the stream was completely iced over and unmoving. The fisher trotted out with considerable confidence, but before he had covered a third of the distance, he was stopped by an ominous creak beneath his feet. A thin, jagged thread showed abruptly white on the black surface. He began to back away cautiously. Through the dimness, he saw that the stiffening wind had lifted a ripple of waves on the bay, and shattered its fragile skin. Rapidly, the new ice was breaking up. He jumped as the crack before him extended itself, jagged sideways, then branched, creating a pattern of white filaments. The fisher turned and leaped, but his claws slipped, and he went down with a crack that split the ice and plummeted him into the water.

He was delighted to find the water considerably warmer than the air. He floated for a moment, his head clear of the surface, then pushing the floating chunks out of his way, struck out for the shore. Climbing out proved to be a problem as, time after time, the ice crumbled beneath him. Finally he swam slowly upstream. The center channel was mostly clear now, and he had no trouble breaking the few crystal bridges still spanning the dark water. He was beginning to tire, when he found himself nearing a pool below a swift, rocky riffle. The swift current had kept the pool nearly clear, and he was easily able to plunge through the thin ice that rimed the banks and to plod ashore.

The ache had returned to his thighs, and he was limping badly as he shook water from his coat. Awkwardly, he moved toward the old man's clearing. He had begun to feel some trepidation about the porcupines, for he knew that a successful kill depended on his being able to move faster than the animal's barbed tail. But the simple, obvious answer to his hunger did not strike him until he was opposite the cabin.

Slipping across the clearing to the side of the hen roost, he went up the wire and eased along the top rail. The mesh was sagging and loose, in places pulled almost free of the rusty staples. The fisher settled on a spot near the roof of the roost where a narrow rent showed. He hooked his claws beneath the mesh, bunched his shoulders, and heaved. The wire tore, opening a gap through which he slid with ease. The chickens awoke at the noise, muttering to each other sleepily.

The rooster came fully awake as the dark shadow blotted out the pale moonlit rectangle of the door. He shot from his perch with a terrified gabble, blundered into the three hens, and sent them squawking to the floor. For a moment, the fisher was lost in a welter of buffeting wings. He sat back and waited. Directly in front of him, a panic-stricken hen ran in tight, aimless circles. The fisher barely had to stretch his neck to grasp her by the head. Her body was still jerking convulsively as he flowed out of the roost, up and through the gap and toward the black screen of trees.

He had covered half the distance to safety, when a movement to his right pulled him around. The old man was staring at him along the barrel of a rifle. He understood the deadly power of the weapon now and crouched lower, waiting for the impact of the bullet. But none came. As he watched, the old man lowered the rifle. The fisher gripped the hen more tightly by the neck, threw a harsh, warning snarl at the Indian, and stalked away.

The old man watched him cross the open ground. He saw the fisher was limping badly and felt concern. Something had transformed the animal's tolerance of him into a rage, for there was no mistaking the naked hate that had flared from the fisher's eyes. Immediately, he thought of the trapper, wondering if he might be behind the injury that had sent the fisher raiding the hen roost.

The Indian shivered, wishing the snow would come to break this penetrating cold. He stepped inside, thinking that tomorrow he must find some way to strengthen the chicken run.

The carcass of the hen, which the fisher dragged back and ate in his den, lasted long enough for him to regain nearly all his strength. After that, hunting offered no immediate problems.

Strangely, as soon as he was able, he began to watch the trapper. In the week following his arrival, the man had stayed near the cabin, working to put it in shape for the winter. He had cleaned the inside of mouse nests and porcupine-gnawed pieces of old, sweat-stained furniture, swept the spiders out of the corners and the bat droppings from the floor, and cut a fragrant, fresh mattress of balsam fir for the rough, wooden bunk. He had chinked the walls with fresh clay and moss, and had restacked the woodpile. Four hours every day he spent woodcutting, building up his stock for the winter. On the afternoon the fisher returned, he was scrambling across the roof, prying up loose shingles, and spreading rolls of thick, waterproof birch bark beneath them.

The fisher had left his den early. Inevitably, it seemed, his trail had led him toward the pond, and now he crouched within the shadowed branches at the edge of the infertile crescent, staring across the greenish ice. He could see the man quite clearly. He looked for the rifle, but its slender, blued outline was not among the multitude of shapes around the cabin. Impulsively, and with a certain feeling of recklessness, he dropped down from the trees and trotted out into the sunshine.

The man saw the animal move, and a frown formed over his eyes. A killer as efficient as the fisher in the vicinity of his trapline could become a serious menace. Slowly, he eased himself off the roof and around to the cabin door. He slipped inside, grabbed his rifle, and levered a cartridge into the barrel. But when he returned, the animal was gone.

He waited a full five minutes before climbing back to the roof. By the time he reached it, the fisher was out in the open, twenty feet from the original position. Blurting an oath, the trapper jumped down and went for his rifle again. Instantly, the fisher faded out of sight. Cursing, the man took the rifle to the roof with him, propping it precariously against the tin chimney. As soon as he moved away from it, the fisher eased into view.

The game went on for an hour. Each time he moved out of reach of the rifle, the fisher appeared. Each time he lunged for it, the fisher slipped back out of sight. Finally, after missing his grip and sending the rifle clattering to the ground, the trapper gave up and contented himself with shouting curses. For his part, the fisher was enjoying himself immensely, sitting happily in the sun, hating the man for all he was worth, and snarling with bared fangs each time the trapper snapped an oath at him.

It was late afternoon when the man finally came down from the roof and picked up the rifle. The fisher dropped back under cover immediately, and through a dense screen of needles, saw the man plod around the pond toward him. He did not know whether the trapper was coming to hunt him, but he felt that the wise course was to leave the area, and quickly.

* * *

II

IN THE TRANQUIL DARK beyond the den, a single snowflake fell. It drifted down the night like a tiny, silver butterfly, dancing and sliding until it touched the ground. There it lay in crystal perfection. The earth below tried to melt it away, but the week of cold had drained the soil of heat, and so the snowflake rested, white and pure, waiting for a twin to fall from the sky.

The fisher awoke to warmth; glorious, enveloping warmth that nudged his mind back to sleep each time it reached toward consciousness. The next sensation was silence, a huge, friendly silence that held sounds captive in its soft interior; and, finally, there was the light, pearly and dim, a substance without shadows that gently tickled his eyelids.

He opened his eyes. Blinking, he stepped forward to inspect the white mass of snow at the mouth of the den. He jerked back as his nose touched the fluff, surprised by its coldness, and flicked out his tongue to clear the slight powdering of crystals from his muzzle. The cool wetness pleased him, and he nipped up a mouthful, rolling it on his tongue and letting it trickle down his throat. Then, he drew a deep breath, half closed his eyes, and plunged head and shoulders into the cottony drift, burrowing quickly toward the expanding light.

He emerged to a sun-bright snowfall.

Directly above him a vast deck of clouds was split transversely by a narrow rift through which the sunlight poured, turning the falling snowflakes into a sparkling shower. It caught in the blanketed branches of the trees, transforming all the soft autumn colors into vital, winter contrasts: woodsy greens and browns and slates grew black, the whites and buffs and yellows bright, and every shadow clasped an undertone of piercing blue. Then, while he watched, the cloud cover closed, and the air took on a milky opalescence.

He inhaled deeply, enjoying the fresh crispness in the air. It slid smoothly into his lungs, invigorating and clean. The ledge to his right was thick with snow, which the light, onshore breeze had banked against the back wall. He drew back into the den and began to clear out the entrance, turning sharply right as he came back into the open, then half burrowed, half tramped a narrow, packed pathway along the inner edge of the ledge.

Swiftly, then, he climbed to the ridge, the click of his claws clear, yet oddly muted in the soft stillness. He cocked his ears about, but heard nothing—or rather he heard the silence, for it was tangible, pressing down on the sleeping lake.

And suddenly, his joy in living overflowed. He raced along the ridge in a wild, ecstatic dance. He snapped at the snowflakes, he batted them, and then he stalked them as they fell and pounced on them with a high and silly shriek. He plunged into a powdery drift banked thickly against a patch of frozen milkweed and burst twisting skyward in a violent eruption of snow and broken stems. He bounded for the shattered jack pine, shot to the top of the lightning split, and stood, his feet bunched together, rocking back and forth like a flying squirrel. And then he was down again and rolling through the snow. He became the hunter, stalking a white-draped milkweed. He became the hunted, dodging and somersaulting to throw the attacking toadflax off his trail. And finally, he simply ran in a circle and chased his own tail.

Within the next few weeks the fisher studied the myriad lessons of winter well. He learned to outwit the rabbits and the ermine, not by hunting them, but their shadows. He discovered that though a white-furred animal fades away against a wall of snow, its shadow seldom does. Only in mist or the new moon's darkness is the camouflage complete. And even then the black accents of the fur or the dark gleam of an eye will betray the masquerader to a hunter that has trained himself to see.

He learned the language of the tracks, written fleetingly across the impermanent face of the snow. The tiny marks of deer mice crisscrossed everywhere, small and birdlike, the thin streak of the pendant tail cutting like a knife edge between each set of tightly grouped prints. Occasionally the paired footmarks of a weasel paralleled them, measuring a foot in each bound, and ending often in a large hole beside a small hole in a drift where the mouse had dived for safety, only to find that the weasel could burrow as well as he. The martens left soft, oval two-inch tracks as they moved from tree to tree, usually in tight pursuit of the crescent-shaped groups of prints put down by fleeing squirrels. The deer punched their strange, split-hooved signature across the open patches, and it was some time before the fisher realized that the two-legged tracks had been left by a four-legged beast, for as they threaded through the trees, the deer carefully placed each hoof on the mark of the hoof before, as if the front and rear halves of the animals were two distinct creatures, the one treading carefully in the other's steps. Surprisingly, the wolves following them walked in much the same way, placing each paw almost directly over the print of the paw in front. He learned to recognize the huge, fuzzy pads of the lynx, the chunky, triangular mark of the mink, and the strange, paw-studded, eight-inch gutters left lining the steep stream banks by the sliding clowns of the north, the river otters.

It took him several days to unravel the enormous oval prints to the west of the lake, and the equally strange giant diamonds to the east, but finally he discovered them to be the snowshoe markings of the trapper on the one hand, and the old Ojibway on the other. Slowly, his encyclopedia of winter lore filled.

It snowed daily for a week after the first fall, piling enormous, powdery drifts in every clearing. The light winds kept the lake surface relatively clear, swirling the snow into hummocks that changed each day. Occasionally, the antediluvian shadows of fish could be seen, clustered in serried ranks below the clear, windswept windows of the ice. Unexpectedly, there was a thaw that lasted only a few hours before a chill northern blast battered it into submission. But it stayed long enough to fill the snow with moisture, packing it into a heavy blanket that would not move till spring. Only then did the fish drift down to their winter holes, patiently waiting for the vernal sun to open up their icebound catacombs. It snowed, and snowed again. The wind whisked the new falls dizzily over the solid base, sculpturing the masses into twisted ridges, undercuts, and sweeping plastic curves. Warm sunlight licked across the surface, leaving a fragile crust. And then, the skies would cloud, fresh snow would whisper down, and the rhythmic ritual would be repeated.

Every change had its repercussions throughout the animal world. The timid red-back voles became raiders, pilfering the storehouses of the squirrels and taking to the trees to steal the mushrooms left drying in the crotches. The snowshoe rabbits grew bolder, sitting in the open and trusting to their coloration for protection while they stripped the dormant willow and alder buds. The whitetail deer forsook the safety of their individual hiding places to herd together and crop the low-hanging birches. Even the fisher found he was starting his hunt earlier every day, to take advantage of the low-angled, shadow-casting sun. By the end of November he was leaving his den with half an hour of sunlight still left in the western sky.

At sunset, on just such an afternoon, the fisher came

down the ridge. The woods were very still, and he ambled through them casually, pausing now and then to draw a deep breath and relish the chill and frothy effervescence of the air. Light caught the edges of a complicated net of tracks, and he trotted over to investigate. The prints showed the story of a chase. A snowshoe rabbit had been flushed by a fox, whose huge prints the fisher had seen before, but not on this side of the lake. The sprayed cascades of snow bespoke the strenuous swings and jogs of the pursuer, and the pockmark of a hole in a soft drift showed where the rabbit had finally plunged. There the fox had paced back and forth, marking the snow with its neat, round prints. The fisher suspected they were those of the big, silver vixen living east of the lake—he knew of no other prints so large—so he trotted north, curious to watch her hunt.

He heard the fox before he saw her. A faint, steady whimpering caught his ears a half mile above the beaver dam. He slowed his pace and edged forward. The fisher saw at once it was the magnificent vixen from east of the lake, but try as he might, he could not make out what she was doing. He could only see the broad outlines of her silhouette and her hunched movements against the snow.

She was chewing something, and chewing hard, using the heavy grinding molars in the back of her jaw. And as she chewed, she whimpered in a steady, aching whine that sent a tremor down the fisher's back. Every few minutes she would stop and lay her head flat along the snow. Then she would start to gnaw once more, and the whines would come until, with almost a sob, she would break away and rest again.

The fisher saw her come slowly to a sitting position, her front legs spread out before her. Straining, she threw her body backward, but her front right paw would not lift off the ground. The fisher stared intently, trying to see what held her. Suddenly, she poised herself, then threw her weight back with all the strength she possessed. The fisher heard a brittle sound, and the vixen toppled with a high yelp of pain. She lay gasping in the snow, her eyes rolled back and her shoulders shivering, then came to her feet, and hobbling on three legs, staggered from the clearing, unmindful of the blood that marked her trail.

The fisher padded forward. The snow where she had first lain was fouled with blood, but the fisher had no eyes for it. He was staring instead at a bright, gleaming crescent of metal with a short anchoring chain. And in its jaws, a thing he could not comprehend: the foot of the vixen from the ankle to the toe, drenched with blood and with pale, creamy pieces of tattered tendon and fascia hanging like streamers from the severed bone.

12

The fisher tried to read the evidence of the tracks for the meaning of what he had seen. There were two sets of prints entering the open ground, the vixen's, and to the west, the huge ovals of the trapper's snowshoes. Both led directly toward a spindly tamarack, though the trapper's tracks ended halfway, obliterated by large, sweeping marks. A large slice of meat, frozen and dark, dangled from a high, out-jutting limb. The rumpled snow beneath showed how the vixen had jumped, and jumped again, straining for the meat, until finally, her foot had touched and triggered the snow-covered trap.

The trap itself meant little to the fisher. Vaguely, he recognized it as an object he had seen before. He sniffed it, bristling at the taint of metal underlying the blood. It did not look dangerous, but somehow, it made the fisher intensely apprehensive. The apparent strength with which it held the tattered remnant of the fox was disturbing, and even as he inspected it, the urge to leave the thing strictly alone grew in him.

The trail of snowshoe prints leading northward caught his eye, and he swung into line with them. For a while they paralleled the lakeshore, then stopped in a series of the odd sweeping marks at the edge of another small clearing. Several yards beyond this point the bottom branches of a young spruce had been hacked away haphazardly, and the intense, skunky smell of the resin filled the air. From the middle branches, again just beyond reach of a leaping fox, hung a gobbet of frozen deer meat. Beneath, the snow was smooth, not unnaturally so; it might well have been laid out by a gentle wind. But there was one unreal note that jarred the fisher's sense of the rightness of things. Despite the damage done above, there was no debris on the snow's face, no needles, no chips or crumbs of bark. So, when he eased himself forward, he did so slowly and with great caution, his eyes and nose locked to the ground. He did not know exactly what he was searching for, but when it came, he recognized it instantly—the faint, sharp tang of metal from below the surface of the snow. He paused, considering, then as carefully as he had advanced, he retreated, placing each paw in the print it had made before.

Twice more he discovered a similar setup in tiny clearings piercing the body of the forest near the shore. Each time he investigated, and each time he was stopped by the unmistakable smell of metal. Then the trail swung away from the lake and toward the flying squirrels' home ground. Within minutes, he found a new and puzzling structure in the snow. Obviously, it was artificial, though the fisher did not yet connect it directly with the trapper. It had been built from straight branches chopped from larger timber. A clutter of aromatic chips lay a short distance away, where the butts had been hacked to a point.

The cubby, for such the structure was called, had been formed by driving the poles into the ground, each snugged tightly against the next like a palisaded wall. The finished construction was remarkably sturdy, for all its simplicity, and extremely simple in shape: a circular pocket of tightly wedged stakes, with an opening at one side framing a narrow, but passable entrance to the interior. A small piece of meat was tied to the stake facing the entrance, and a few tiny chunks scattered on the snow outside.

The fisher circled the cubby, sniffing the snow before each step. He wrinkled his nose in distaste. The bait appealed to him not at all, for dead meat still held no charms, but his curiosity over the purpose of the structure drew him on. Dead center in the opening, he once again caught the hint of steel and backed off slowly. Dimly, he began to perceive a purpose to the structure; it offered food to any animal hungry enough to take it, but to reach the food, the animal had to pass through the entrance, and that meant passing over the hidden, waiting steel.

There were two more cubbies in the tract of trees between the lake and the nesting ground of the flying squirrels. The second held an ermine. His struggles had roiled the snow between the stakes until, after an hour, he had dropped in exhaustion. He dragged himself painfully to his feet when the fisher appeared, staggering slightly under the weight of the clinging trap and chain, then dropped with a half-hearted hiss of anger. The fisher worked slowly forward, but the only steel he smelled was from the trap on the weasel's leg. When finally he stood above the creature, it scarcely looked at him.

The fisher devoured his kill quickly. He left the foreleg still intact between the jaws, not wishing to come in contact with the evil-smelling steel, and though the hint of man smell about the cubby disturbed him at first, well before he finished the meal, he was more or less reconciled to it. He even felt a certain grudging approval toward the device that held prey so conveniently in one place for killing.

Farther on he came upon a marten, frozen solid. He nudged the body, firmly enough to flip it over, and saw the familiar semicircle of a trap fixed around the marten's foreleg. The chain was taut, a rigid tether from the trap to a staple driven deeply into the roots of the tree. A few inches in front of the dead animal's nose, a stake had been driven into the snow, and to the top were stapled several streamers of the kind used for neck-banding geese. The bright red and yellow ribbons of plastic fluttered in the evening breeze, incongruously gay against the somber grays and mauves.

The fisher tried to puzzle out the story of the marten's death. It had not struggled in the trap. The tracks showed how the animal had come down the tree at a dead run, fascinated by the carnival dance of the gaudy ribbons. The trap had sprung and tripped the marten halfway to its goal. The supple neck was twisted sharply back. Still the fisher was perplexed, for he simply could not visualize how a cleverly placed trap could tumble a running animal. Actually, it mattered little. The marten was in a trap and dead, and that was fact enough to clinch the fisher's growing wariness of these strange devices scattered so freely about his territory.

He discovered another beribboned stake two hundred yards to the east, then nothing until he reached the stream that flowed beneath slender ice bridges north from the lake. The man's tracks led toward a natural pocket of rock and dwarf juniper, facing an open rill where the faintly steaming water flowed too swiftly to allow the formation of ice. The fisher nosed about the area, drawn by the positive scent of fish, but when he tracked it to its source—a fish head lying beneath a mat of shrubs flanked by two lichened rocks—he stopped, suspicious, straining for the smell of steel. And he found it, faint but sure.

He discovered two more traps between the first set and the northern limit of his hunting grounds. Each was baited with fish heads and faced an open riffle of water. The second had been sprung. A trail of large mink tracks led from the edge of the stream, downwind to a point where the mink had picked up the smell of fish, then arrowed directly toward the trap. It must have been an old and wily mink, clever enough to recognize the danger the moment its paws touched the pan, for it had lunged back so quickly only two toes on the outside of the foot had been caught. The fisher could see the animal had wasted little time in struggling, but had set to work quickly to gnaw itself free. The red-threaded trail led straight back to the water, and the fisher noticed with interest the irregularity of the paw prints. Three claws of the right rear foot were missing, evidence of an ancient injury that had taught the brutal lesson in escape.

The fisher prodded the bait, but found long-dead fish as repugnant as dead meat. He stared northward along the disappearing line of snowshoe tracks, trying to decide whether to follow farther. But he was at the limit of his hunting range, and north lay unknown, unexplored territory. The combination of hidden traps and unknown ground was more than he was willing to face.

Later, while he slept, a blizzard hit. It was a minor storm, the first of the year, and one that caused remarkably little discomfort, for it carried neither sleet nor killing cold, satisfying itself with dumping down a few more tons of snow and rearranging that already fallen. Within forty-eight hours—except for a few new baroques on the lake and in the clearings—there was little evidence that it had ever been.

The day after the storm, the fisher burrowed from his den, pushing through the soft snow plugging his runway along the back of the ledge. Under the glare of the afternoon sun, the snow had softened, then stiffened to a thin, hard crust when the sun went westering. The fisher was delighted to find that, though it bulged and cracked from the press of his body beneath, the crust held its own weight, forming a roof above his walkway from the entrance to the roots, and making his den windproof and invisible.

He came down the ridge and began to hunt. Before

he even reached the trapline, he flushed and killed a rabbit. He fed, trotted through the late afternoon to see what changes the blizzard had wrought in his world. He cocked his ears and froze as he made out the muffled swish of snowshoes making steadily in his direction. Swiftly and silently, he dropped back into the shadows. The trapper appeared, hunching along with the peculiar stiff-legged gait of the experienced snowshoer. Between the heavy beard and the thick, wolverine fur edging of the parka's hood, the fisher could see a patch of pale skin, and the dark glitter of the man's eyes. He tensed when the man stopped and knelt to examine the fisher's big paw prints. For an endless minute, he stared along the fisher's trail, then grunted to his feet and swung rhythmically southeastward toward the marsh, leaving behind a cloud of frozen breath and the sharp smell of sweat.

Impulsively, the fisher followed until he could see the trapper's bulky form through the screen of trees. He watched the man kneel and work at the snow twice before he reached the marsh, and in each case found it was a trap the man was tending, clearing the snow away from the buried baits and resetting the traps so that only a thin crusting of snow covered the waiting jaws. Each time, he saw the man brush the area over the trap with an owl's wing, then blank out the big ovals with an evergreen bough.

He stayed within the trees while the man moved across the marsh, visiting several of the shrouded muskrat domes, and watched curiously as the bowed figure swung a short-handled ax against the ice. When the man finished, the fisher slipped out into the bleakness. He could make little of what he found, a swiftly freezing hole above the muskrat's underwater entrance and a pole pushed through it to the bottom. Beyond his ken were the submerged, open jaws of the small trap chained to the pole, waiting to grasp and hold the soft-furred rodent underwater till it drowned.

As often as he could in the next two weeks, he trailed the squat, broad-shouldered form, learning the location of every trap to the west of the lake. The trapper kept his operations strictly within the limits set by the old Ojibway, partly because he was a basically honest man, but mostly because it had been years since a trapper had been anywhere near the area, and the game was exceedingly plentiful and unwary. The trapline ran from the beaver dam to the north shore of the lake, up to the favored ground of the martens and squirrels, then east to the mink dens along the northerly stream. The fisher never followed it beyond his own territory, but picked it up again where it re-entered his preserve two miles to the west. It ran due south from there, then began a slow swing east, a mile beyond the trapper's cabin, looping through the triangle of second-growth timber, up to the muskrat houses on the marsh, then in a shallow, concave curve back to the beaver pond.

Bit by bit, the fisher began to make the trapline his personal hunting domain. He used it casually at first, killing a trapped animal on those few nights when regular hunting proved more difficult than usual. But the deceptive ease of it was much too tempting. Before two weeks were up, the trapline had become his sole source of food. He was soon making rounds as regularly as the trapper, picking up each night from where he had broken off the night before. Anything that moved, foxes, ermine, martens, he considered fair game, but any animal already dead he left alone. In time he would eat dead flesh freely; for the present he was still too close to his mother's teachings and thus, once he had eaten, he had no further reason for killing. After his meal, he would work his way along the line, checking on the old sets and inspecting any new ones the trapper had installed. Gradually, he began to build up a remarkable store of knowledge about the trapper's ways.

The trapper was growing very angry. Day by day he watched the mounting evidence that a fisher was looting his line, no longer sporadically, but with nightly regularity. As yet he held no great grudge against the animal itself, for he knew that the fisher was merely taking an easy shortcut to hunting. He was simply intensely annoyed that he should be saddled with a raider on his line, this of all years. He had started late, and though the wealth of wildlife in this inaccessible area held promise of a bumper crop of peltries, he knew he would lose seriously if he did not destroy the animal. And so he decided to double trap the sets, hoping as he worked that the fisher was still young and inexperienced.

That night, in the last hour before dawn, his efforts came to fruition. The moon had set early and the woods were dim beneath a jeweled web of stars. The fisher padded south from the blackness beneath the evergreens into the lesser blackness below the birch and aspens near the ridge. He was tense and unhappy, angry from a night's poor hunting along the trapline. In every set he visited, the traps were either unsprung or held prey already dead. Foolishly he had gone from set to set, hoping each time that the next would hold a meal, instead of breaking away to use his own superb hunting skills in the open forest. But he was spoiled and just now becoming aware that it was far too late to try the easily hunted spruce grouse grounds.

The silhouette of a long-eared owl drifted across the stars, then plummeted behind a line of trees. Almost instantly, the sharp shriek of an ermine cut the stillness, followed by the bright, musical clink of chain. The fisher swerved and bounded through the drifts so swiftly that a sudden rooster tail of snow spurted beneath his flying feet. He burst into the open in time to see the owl shoot skyward with a trapped ermine in its talons. Three feet up straight they went, then the chain jangled taut, and the ermine was wrenched from the owl's grasp. The owl looked down in surprise, caught a glimpse of the fisher racing in from the side, and gave up his prize.

The ermine was lying stunned within the cubby, the blood streaks from the owl's talons a sullen red against the silver coat. Before the confused creature could collect himself, the fisher was on him. The fisher felt no apprehension over being so close to the structure, for all his experience told him the sets were safe once the trap had been sprung. But finally he decided the cubby was too cramped for comfort, so grasping the ermine by the neck he began to back out, lifting the little body clear of the snow. The chain rattled after him, then snagged. He threw his weight against it, leaning back as the chain went taut. It held for an instant, then pulled loose, sending him staggering. He was just regaining his balance when he felt the trap trigger.

Afterward, he had a surprisingly clear recollection of the moment, first of something round and hard beneath the snow, which gave slightly under the pressure of his foot, then of the muffled click of the trigger and a barely audible swish as the jaws sprang through the thin crust and bit deeply into his right hind foot. The sudden slash of pain dropped him to the ground, twisting and fighting. He arched his back and heaved, and felt the chain slacken as the clog, a four-foot length of heavy birch slithered toward him. He heaved again, pulling the monstrous weight diagonally across the mouth of the cubby. Then, as if he were in the depths of some hideous nightmare, he felt another hard roundness give beneath his left forepaw, heard the treacherous click, and fell with a second trap cutting into the muscles of his foreleg.

Hopelessness swept through him as he lay on the disturbed snow, swiveling his head from one side to the other, staring at the harsh chains anchoring him to two heavy lengths of log. He was spread-eagled across the shadowed mouth of the cubby. Then, the hopelessness faded as he pushed himself to his feet, grimly determined to fight the traps with every ounce of strength in his body. As he tensed to lunge, he looked to the sky and saw the stars dying, their brilliance flagging under the hint of dawn. It was then that he knew he must hurry, for his danger would be increased a hundredfold beneath the revealing light of day.

13

THE MAN had placed the traps well, using every trick in his repertoire. The heavy clogs had been buried completely, and the chains threaded underneath the snow before stapling. To hide the traps, he had lifted rectangles of thin crust with a slim birchwood paddle, sliding them over the waiting jaws when the traps were in place, and covering the telltale cracks with a dusting of snow brushed in with an owl's wing. The weasel trap had been set well within the entrance of the cubby to force the fisher to back out with his prize. And each of the large unbaited outer traps had been laid so that no matter which one the fisher stepped in, he would automatically pull away from the clog toward the jaws of the other. With two traps, the man knew he stood a good chance of disabling the fisher effectively enough to prevent him gnawing his way out. And, to his credit, the set had worked exactly as he had planned.

The fisher lay resting on the snow. He had not given up, would never give up, even when the trapper came to kill him. But he had been struggling for nearly a half hour, closing his mind to the pain as he wrenched and fought against the traps. His right rear paw was caught between the toes and the ankle. At first, the trap had been higher, but the jaws had slipped, ripping his skin under the tremendous strain. Now, with the flesh of his foot swelling, and the excess blood suffusing into it past the choked arteries, he could make no further headway. The jaws bit cruelly into the turgid flesh, and every new attempt seemed only to increase the trap's hold.

A slight flicker of movement brought his eyes around toward the line of tree hiding the dawn. A gray shadow drifted through the pallid light, a shadow that shifted shape a dozen times before it finally solidified into the hulking form of a timber wolf.

The fisher tensed his stomach muscles, and with a tremendous effort, managed to draw his body into a tight arch, wrenching one of the thick logs through the snow sufficiently to slacken the chains. Then, reaching out with his right paw, he hooked his claws into a ridge under the papery bark and drew his body and the other clog two feet closer. The strain sent new agonies slashing though his numbed limbs, but he persisted until he had gained enough slack to enable him to stand and turn to either side. He lay back with lungs heaving and stared at the wolf. The wolf stared back dispassionately.

Then the wolf ambled slowly forward, his massive shoulders rolling in a deceptively loose-limbed gait. Gradually, he began to circle, trotting around the fisher in a slow spiral that brought him closer with every turn. The fisher refused to turn with him and chance becoming entangled in the chains; instead, he worked himself laboriously toward the cubby, using it as protection for his back. It was merely a delaying action, for he knew that without speed and the chance to retire to the safety of the treetops, he did not have a hope of outfighting the huge and patient killer.

The wolf made a fast feint from the side. The fisher whirled to face him and surged forward until the chains pulled him up short, screaming and snapping at the empty air while the wolf dodged out of reach. Quickly, the big killer darted around the cubby and bored in from the opposite side. The fisher nearly lost his precarious footing when he hit the limit of the chains and was yanked to an abrupt stop, but the gleam of his bared fangs made the wolf draw back to reconsider. He was not afraid, for fear was as foreign to his make-up as to the fisher's. More than anything, he was surprised to find the fisher still so fast when so badly hampered. He knew he could take the animal in a straight fight, but he also knew the fisher would cut him up rather badly before he died, and the swiftly waxing light told him it was already too late to call the pack together from around the lake for a team attack. And so he took the simple, obvious alternative. He decided to watch and wait while cold and pain did their debilitating work.

The old Ojibway dragged himself from bed. Stretch and yawning away his few rheumatic twinges, he cursed as he dressed, wishing the rooster would learn that the first brightening of the light no longer meant the sun was only moments away. Since the snow had come, the fool cock had lost his sense of timing completely, waking the old man anywhere up to an hour before sunrise. The Indian sighed as he splashed a palmful of water in his face, rumpled his already sleep-rumpled hair, and poked the banked fires in stove and fireplace alive again. Then he picked up his parka and a long-bladed ice chisel, and stepped out into the frozen air. Ten minutes later, he stamped out of the outhouse and straight toward the bay.

The burgeoning light outlined the small but sturdy lean-to, anchored in the ice above his five fishing holes. Swiftly, he broke the thin skeins of ice and checked the lines. Three were untouched, the fourth heavy with a fat, three-pound whitefish, and the last pulled tight by an ugly twelve inches of burbot in full spawning regalia. The sight surprised him, for it was still a fortnight to the normal spawning season, and the fish was a female, gravid with eggs. He smiled faintly as he reset the lines. Of the few pounds of butter he had bought that fall in a moment of self-indulgence, there was just enough left for one good feast of burbot roe on hot, buttered bannock. He decided that as soon as he got back to the cabin, he would set to work on a batch of fresh sora dough.

A rising flash of white above the trees snagged his attention, and he glanced up, curious to see what was flying so high, so early. His eyes caught and held a high-winging gyrfalcon as it floated in a drifting spiral skyward. It had been years since one of the big falcons had come from the arctic for the winter, so it was not until the huge bird had settled toward the windbreak of evergreens rimming the spit of land across from his cabin that the old man recognized the strong, pointed wings and the long, narrow tail of the most royal of hunting birds. Intrigued, he raced up the shore, threw the fish inside the cabin door, then slipped on his snowshoes and struck out across the drifted ice.

The gyrfalcon glared at him coldly as he rounded the spit, ruffling its magnificent gray and white plumage and spreading its broad wings threateningly. For a long moment, bird and man eyed each other, then the great bird sprang skyward with a rush of feathers and click of talons, and beat on rapid wings toward the sentinel spruce.

It was the first time the old man had been this far out on the lake since the snow and, as every year, he was vaguely shocked at the utter barrenness of the marsh, the vast emptiness now that the wild rice and burr reeds were down. It was a whitened world of curves and flats with scarcely any focal points on which to fix the eyes. But gradually, he became aware that this year there was a difference, an incongruity in the huge irregularity of the scene. It took him a few minutes to pin the cause down to a series of short, sharp verticals before several of the snow-draped muskrat domes.

He recognized the purpose of the icebound poles immediately, though he was surprised to find the trapper using such a complex set for muskrat. A glance about the area showed him why. The ice was totally devoid of push-ups, the tiny grass and reed way stations muskrats build above holes gnawed when the ice grows so thick it threatens to cut off their normal food supply of mussels, pond-weed roots, and tubers. That there were none was proof that the big rodents were not, as yet, coming out to forage on the shore. Evedently, the trapper felt it was worth the extra effort of maintaining pole traps to catch the muskrat when their coats were prime, before the deepening ice ushered in the hungry days. It saddened the old man to think of how few of the muskrats would survive the year.

Yet, there was one consolation in what he saw, which gave, if not a glimmer of hope, at least an easing of his depression. The trapper had refrained from splitting open the domes and laying traps inside. And the law was very clear on that point. Trapping muskrats in their push-ups was quite legal. Setting traps in the domes or in any other burrow or structure where the rodents had laid out bedding materials was definitely not. Obviously, the trapper was staying exactly within the limits set by regulations. His curiosity piqued, the old Ojibway strode toward the blue-green wall of spruce edging the far curve of the marsh. Breakfast could wait, and now was as good a time as any to see what caliber of trapper his neighbor was.

The big wolf lay stretched full length on the snow, just beyond the fisher's extreme reach, his head on his paws. The light grew steadily, washing through the quiet clearing until the first ray of sun split the top branches of the eastern line of trees. The fisher recoiled inwardly from its brilliance, even while yearning for its warmth to come and drive away the deadly, aching cold. Each time the wolf stirred, he lunged forward, snarling, but every movement drained him a fraction more.

The wolf was growing edgy too. Though he was not exclusively a night creature, the sun jabbed an anxious needle along his nerves. He did not like these leafless limbs that let in so much of the sky, and the desire to move back north beneath the shadowed masses of the evergreens grew into a tangible ache. Abruptly, he rose, tensed his haunches, and settled his feet firmly in readiness to spring. Then, in a fractional lull between the fisher's snarls, he heard a sound that stopped him.

At first, the fisher was unaware of the change, for his ears were filled with his own towering rage. But when he saw the sudden shift in the big wolf's attention, the swift, sideward roll of the dark eyes, and the intent, backward flick of the ears, the hisses died in his throat and he cocked his own softly rounded ears forward. The sound came first as a faint undertone to the chirping of the birds, then grew and unfolded until it blossomed into the soft, rhythmical swish of snowshoes.

The wolf moved so swiftly he seemed to flicker, racing across the snow toward an alder thicket. He ran belly to the ground, not skulkingly, but with tail high and eyes bright, stretching his big body into an impressive, ground-eating lope. He slipped gracefully between the downcast branchlets and blended into the morning shadows.

Tense, alert, and determined to fight, the fisher was turned toward the dimness beneath the sun-touched trees. Vaguely, he made out a figure, striding past him along an aisle between the trees, a hundred feet away. At the sight of the man, the fisher threw himself into a paroxysm of effort, wrenching and twisting his body against the steel. He had a quick impression of the man's head swiveling, then the mists of exhaustion closed over him and he dropped, panting weakly, to the snow. When he looked up, it was into the infinitely warm and compassionate depths of the Ojibway's eyes.

The old man's brows lifted when he spotted the wolf's tracks and saw the story of the two cautious sallies, the waiting, and the final, swift flight. He was sure the big gray animal was somewhere near, but he knew it was pointless to look, for the wolf was the north's supreme master of winter camouflage. His eyes went to the two traps fastened around the fisher's legs, and he frowned, angered at the size the trapper had used; they were number fours, big, heavy traps large enough to hold an otter. The fisher would be lucky, he thought, to come out of it without a broken leg.

The old man did not act immediately, for by the rules of this vast and empty land a man did not touch the trapline of another. It took a conscious effort for him to overcome the ingrained habits of a lifetime. He found some consolation in the traditions of his own people, where one who saved another's life was responsible for that life. I will try to set you free, he thought as he strode forward; I will see if I can calm you enough. But if you are too badly hurt, if your legs are broken or you are crippled, I will kill you, for that will be the most merciful thing I can do.

He could see the rich fur along the fisher's back literally lift as he rustled through the snow and knelt, just beyond the reach of the fangs. The animal lunged at him with a snarl that rose to a scream. He lunged again, and still again, wrenching against the chains. And then, slowly, just perceptibly, the gentle tones of the old man's voice began to seep through to the raging animal. Moment by moment, the frantic thrashing stilled, till the fisher crouched on the snow with his lips drawn back, but his ears cocked forward, listening.

The Indian knew that his next moves were critical. Without breaking the smooth flow of quiet words, he straightened up and slid his hand forward until he gripped the nearer clog. The fisher tensed and glared, but settled back under the strangely calming quality of the man's voice. In that moment, the old Indian moved the wood. The log was hard and heavy, but he lifted it with one hand in a sweeping arc that carefully, but firmly, pulled the fisher's hind leg from beneath him and stretched him helplessly on the snow. The animal went rigid. He tried to arch his back and draw the clod forward to give him slack in the chain, but the old man knelt swiftly, his full weight on the log. He reached for the trap, slipping off his mittens to work his fingers between the jaws. Then, with a bunching of his shoulders, he pressed down and forced the steel apart.

The fisher did not know he had been freed until, as the strain went off his leg, he tumbled in the snow. He stared at the old Ojibway blowing on reddened hands, then at his own leg, numb and nerveless, but free. Slowly, he looked into the seamed copper face, trying to read a meaning there for what he could no longer understand. But he could find no answer. In his mind dwelt only confusion. Man had been the instrument behind his being trapped, and now man was the instrument of his freedom. Man had fired the rifle that had hurt his hip, and yet man had fed and warmed him while he healed after the nightmare of the fire. Unbidden, a flood of images went flickering through his mind, scenes without sequence, without reason.

The old man grunted and massaged his kidneys. He worked his way around to the other side of the fisher, wondering if he could possibly free the animal without having his hands too badly cut up, for he knew the slashing power of the twelve razor-edged incisors in those jaws. He looked down at the graceful form, noticing with approval that though the lips were still wrinkled back, the hackles were down and the green flame was dying in the eyes. He kicked off his snowshoes and began to hunker closer to the animal, working toward the other clog.

At that moment, the fisher made what was possibly the most important discovery of his life. It came to him the instant the man moved upwind, for in the pleasant muskiness, the warm, woodsy scent that overlaid the sweat smell, was the clear message that this man was an individual, a separate creature, a being not to be placed in the collective picture of man. For this man was as unique and different from the hunter and the trapper as he was himself from all others, even the fisher that denned somewhere to the north. And this man, this warm, familiar-smelling creature was part of the best memories he had of the time since coming to the lake.

Later, the old Ojibway was to remember what followed as one of the most satisfying moments of his latter life. He moved very slowly as he neared the fisher. He knew what he was doing was extremely dangerous, that the fisher was quite capable of injuring him severely, even of killing him. Still, he reached for the trap, slipped his fingers between the jaws and pulled, slowly forcing the heavily sprung steel apart. The animal leaned forward, and the old man flinched, expecting to feel the sharp slash of teeth, but the fisher merely pushed his hot, dry nose against the cool flesh, inhaled slightly, then carefully drew his leg free of the gaping jaws. The old Ojibway slumped at the sudden release of tension. The fisher eyed him curiously while he ran a probing tongue over the deep furrows the trap had left in his swollen leg. The man reached out to touch him, but the fisher rumbled softly in his throat. The old Ojibway sat back with a warm chuckle. In spite of everything, the fisher was maintaining his dignity, letting the old man know that he alone would choose when overtures might be made.

For five minutes they rested by each other, the fisher lying calmly in the snow, the man kneeling beside him. Together, they shared the sounds of the waking wood, the saucy jeering of the squirrels, the tipsy slurr of a big, gray jay, and from near the marsh, the weird, electric purr and buzz of a wandering winter flock of snow buntings.

The fisher came to his feet, grunting unhappily as sharp stabs of pain laced through his quickening limbs. The old Ojibway watched closely as he put his weight on first one, then the other injured leg, and slowly began to limp in the direction of the ridge. He heaved a deep sigh of relief to see the animal walk, however painfully, for it would have broken his heart to have to kill the fisher after the moments just past.

It took the old man an hour to return the clearing to its unmarked state. As he moved beneath the trees, brushing out his tracks, he paused and looked back with satisfaction. The body of the ermine was gone and the trap reburied; the clogs were dug beneath the snow again, and his, the fisher's, and the wolf's footprints carefully wiped away. Only the trapper's telltale ovals remained, plodding toward the clearing and away again. He raised his head as he worked, letting the faint warmth of the sun caress his face. Silently, he prayed the trapper would not visit the set until the sun had had sufficient time to lay a thin, hard, obliterating crust over the freshly turned snow.

He swept out his own trail coming in from the marsh for nearly fifty yards, then matching his steps exactly to the earlier prints, worked in a swift swing south. Looking back again at his handiwork, he could see no visible evidence that he had been near the clearing. Next, he picked up the fisher's erratic trail and followed it directly up the ridge, meticulously erasing every sign of the limping footprints with the big, rough diamonds of his snowshoes. Finally, as he stood beneath the sentinel spruce at the point of the ridge, he trampled the snow, removing any indications that the animal had slipped down the root ladder to the ledge.

Suddenly, in a great rush of wings, the gyrfalcon swept majestically from the tree above him. It hung hovering for an instant against the sky, then plummeted earthward in an unbelievable dive that climaxed in the sharp scream of an unlucky snowshoe rabbit. And abruptly, if somewhat gruesomely, the old man realized he had not yet had breakfast.

14

In all it was five days before the fisher quit the den. The pain left his feet within a day and the swelling shortly after. The cuts scabbed over cleanly, but it was days before the tendons he had pulled in his shoulder would bear more than a fraction of his weight. Most of the time he drowsed, escaping from his hunger to the twilit world of sleep. Shortly after sunrise on the third day, he was jerked awake by the whipcrack of a small-caliber rifle. He lay listening intently until the voices of the squirrels and chickadees filtered into his den once more, then relaxed and closed his eyes. Ten minutes later, he was tensed again. He heard a muffled thud, a scraping of leather on wood, then the faint whisper of snowshoes fading away. Cautiously, the fisher hobbled out.

A freshly killed willow ptarmigan lay on the ledge. He nosed the faintly warm body curiously, gripped it by its flopping neck, and dragged it into his den. There, by feeding, resting and feeding again, he devoured the bird to the last bone. Only the feathers remained to join the egg shells heaped in the corner. It was a gift that enabled him to heal in comfort.

The surge of hate he had felt for the Indian the night he had raided the henroost was gone. An earlier sensation had been rekindled. It was not trust, not yet, for the fisher trusted no one but himself. Futhermore, trust was a rare commodity in his world and not a thing given easily by a young hunter, not before a great deal of time had passed. What he gave to the old man was his respect and the willingness to accept what the future offered. And so when hunger finally drove him from his den, it was not toward the trapline but to the Indian's side of the lake that he turned.

At the old man's cabin he came upon a scene that fascinated him. Never had he seen so many animal tracks. From every tree surrounding the cleared ground, the red squirrel prints laced the snow, converging on the big chopping stump near the chicken run. The top of the stump was littered with tiny piles of wild rice kernels, with cranberries, shriveled blueberries and gooseberries, with skunk currants and raisins, seeds and nuts and dozens of small, dark pieces of meat. Two short, round objects were suspended on stiff wires under the eaves. Each was literally bristling with chickadees, hanging at every impossible angle and screeching with excitement as they pecked the mass beneath their feet.

The fisher flowed smoothly toward the woodpile. The rooster, lording over the world of his run, peered myopically at the dark shape, then with a horrified squawk, rocketed through the tiny doorway into the coop. But the fisher paid him little attention. His curiosity was about the things beneath the eaves. He vaulted to the top of the woodpile and rose on his hind legs to sniff while the chickadees scattered.

The round objects were certainly food. The fisher could see seeds and nuts and berries within the grayish, semi-transparent black. What was most puzzling was the distinctly animal smell. He reached out and took a small nip. He tasted animal fat, loaded with nuts and fruit. He spat it out immediately, for this had none of the rich smoothness of fat stripped from around the belly muscles of a kill. This fat had been cooked and melted, and he found it revolting. The birds seemed to love it, for even as he stood spitting the fat taste from his mouth, one of the little gray and black acrobats shot down for a morsel he had rejected.

The sound of wood on wood snapped his attention toward the far corner of the cabin. He crouched warily, listening to the crunch of the old man's boots along the path between the outhouse and the door. The Indian stopped when he came around the corner, staring in surprise as the fisher slipped down the woodpile and across the snow to the trees. The old Ojibway pushed his way inside the cabin, then reappeared with a buff egg cupped in his palm. The fisher uttered a low growl of warning. The man smiled understandingly, walked to the woodpile and balanced the egg on its highest point. He strode down to the lakeshore and set about a quite unnecessary inspection of the overturned canoes, high on their winter rests of poles. From the corner of his eye, he saw the slender shape flicker across to the frozen logs and watched admiringly while the animal opened the fragile shell without spilling a drop.

The fisher finished with his nose deep in the shell.

Suddenly playful, he sat up with it still balanced in place, drew a deep breath, and snorted. The shell arced through the air and rolled on the snow. Feeling quite at ease, he stretched luxuriously, glanced up at the lines of watchful chickadees, then dropped gracefully to the snow.

After that, the old Ojibway's cabin became the focal point of each night's travels. Although the fisher did not meet the Indian directly again, his eye had been caught by a softly silvered glint at the top of the woodpile. He found an egg, nestled in a protected hollow among the logs, with the hen smell still faint upon it. The next evening he made a point of visiting the cabin early. An egg was waiting. The evening after, there was none. But the night following he found another. It became an evening ritual that he looked forward to with great pleasure. He was never resentful, only faintly disappointed when an egg was not waiting, and always delighted to find one there. He would slip around the back corner of the cabin and up the steep slope at the rear of the woodpile, juggle the fragile prize, then remove the top with three precise, razored nips. The shells he dropped at the foot of the woodpile. By morning they would be gone, carried off by deer mice and voles.

The next days and nights were perhaps the most perfect of the entire winter, as the calming hand of the solstice stretched across the sleeping lake. The weather was superb. Each morning the sun rose late, small and immaculate and radiant. And each evening it bedded early, trailing gold and scarlet down the lucent sky. At night the stars looked down through the flames of an aurora that writhed in ripples of green and blue and violet around the northern rim of a caliginous world. And everywhere the air was still, and the scream of the hawk rang out for miles and miles.

The weather was a magnet that gathered up the courage of the timid ones about the lake and drew them from their winter strongholds. It bubbled like wine through the veins of the tiny deer mice, who blinked their shoe-button eyes in the afternoon light and sat back to sing their sweet songs. The waiting weasels watched, then flowed like mist across the snow, the joyful pulse of the hunt beating in their brains. They sprang like ghosts, and the little singers died, scarcely knowing they had been attacked. Yet, even in their dying there was a strange poetry. For as the spark was quenched, the victims gave the gift of life to those who took it from them. Sudden death was the way of life beneath the evergreens, and though each creature preyed upon its neighbor, they formed between them a long and complex chain by which each one sustained the next.

Every afternoon of that unparalleled week the fisher lay on his ledge, drowsing while his coat drank up the heat of the sun. Lazily he watched the deer mice and saw the weasels spring, and heard their triumphant shrieks. As day drifted into evening, he would come down from the ridge to join the hunters himself. Swiftly he regained strength and mobility so that by the last week of December, only during a strenuous chase would the twinges awaken in his shoulder to remind him of what he had suffered.

His thoughts were seldom actively on the trapper, though he was still quite conscious of the man's presence in the area. Unknowingly, he was waiting until he had healed completely. Yet, all the while, it was simply a matter of the proper stimulus to trigger the anger buried in him into action.

It came on Christmas Eve.

The fisher reached the cabin an hour before midnight. Confidently, he loped across the open ground and up the woodpile. There he stopped, his ears cocked alertly to the sound of voices. The old man's was instantly identifiable, gentle and rippling. The other voice had a ring of familiarity too, but one he could not place immediately.

For half an hour, the voices droned on. Gradually, the fisher grew restless, for despite his hopes, there was no egg for him here this night. He was just about to leave when he heard the scrape of feet coming toward the front of the cabin. Swiftly, the fisher dropped to the ground, and faded into the shadows behind the woodpile. The door opened, and a swath of light lay across the trampled snow. The old man stepped into the light. Then, somewhat unsteadily, he walked across to the woodpile and placed an egg carefully in its usual place.

The fisher was just about to trot forward when the second figure appeared. The fisher went rigid as he recognized the broad shoulders and the great, black beard of the trapper. The man stalked forward to stand beside the old Ojibway. His eyes swung around the clearing, day-bright beneath the rustling aurora, then fixed on the bunched sets of prints the fisher had made in his nightly visits to the woodpile. He knelt to examine them and snapped a harsh question at the old man. The Indian stared at the trapper, then without a word, turned and walked back into the cabin. The trapper followed, all traces of unsteadiness gone, and the door snapped shut.

The fisher listened to the rising voices, automatically testing the air and separating the odors left hanging behind. Without doubt the second man was the trapper; the fisher's nose was even more certain than his eyes had been. There was no mistaking the fetid rankness, the hated sweat smell so easily distinguishable from the softer subtlety of the old man. Overlying both was something new, a sharp smell that brought to mind overripe berries, but stronger, much more intense. He tried sorting to the depths of his memory, but could not place it. And so he filed it away, along with the other pleasantly repulsive man smells he found so intriguing.

The voices from inside the cabin changed. The fisher heard the shift in tone and sensed within it a growing tension. Finally, there was a long pause. The trapper slammed out the cabin door, kicked on his snowshoes, and stalked stiff-legged across the pale, frozen face of the lake. The fisher crouched in the shadows, tasting his reawakened rage. Then he started across the clearing, stopping for an instant at the open cabin door. He stared at the old man leaning against the frame, then thrust away again to the north. Later, perhaps, he might think of the old Ojibway and the egg. At the moment, he was ruled by anger, as everything he had felt in the trap and later in his den came surging back to life.

The old Indian caught the glint of green eyeshine and, peering closely, saw the fisher slip away. He recognized the animal more by the way the white band across the shoulders gave the silhouette and odd irregularity than by actually seeing him, for his eyes were still dazzled by the brightness of the cabin and his brain by the alcohol. He raised his hand to his eyes and rubbed them wearily. He knew he had been a fool. Not so much for inviting the trapper to a Christmas supper, for he had been rather ashamed of his surly behavior when the man first had come to the lake. Enough of his faith remained for him to believe in the message of Christmas, and as one of the only two human beings for several hundred miles, he had felt the need to make the gesture. He had been a fool, he thought, for drinking so much of the liquor the man had brought, and even more so for setting out an egg while the trapper was there to see. If he had even taken a moment to think, he would have known the trapper would be harboring suspicions about a set that somehow had seemed slightly different from the way he had laid it and about the sudden disappearance for nearly two weeks of an animal that had been pilfering his trapline. The man was too good a trapper not to add up the clues.

The old man heaved a sigh. The trapper had flatly accused him of interfering with his trapline, had called it unforgivable, and that was true. It had been totally wrong of him. Yet, he had only done what he knew he had to do, and if necessary, would do again.

He lifted his head to the aurora—pale lime, gentle rose, deceptively sharp, electric blue. Tonight it seemed close to the earth. The old man shivered suddenly. There was the smell of change on the wind, a hint of something inevitable coming to sweep away the days and nights of perfect winter, leaving in their place a harsher land, more brutal, more troubled than it had been for all the weeks past.

15

THE FISHER felt the change coming. For over a week, the broad masses of air had lain dormant on the land. Now they were on the move, sweeping downward toward the cities to the south. In their place came a great flood of air bearing a burden of bitter cold. And as the killing cold swirled among the trees, the little ones that lived beneath the snow burrowed deeper, the sleeping birds ruffled up until they looked like feathered pine cones, and even the fisher, warm with movement, felt his fur lift for added insulation.

He picked up the trapline on the bank of the northerly stream. A mink lay dead, a slender length of gleaming fur, near the steaming rush of an open riffle. The fisher circled the body warily, staring at the pale froth of frozen bubbles edging the tight grin that death had drawn on the delicate muzzle.

He sat quietly and considered the body of the mink for some moments. In his mind, a series of associations formed. The mink lay dead and therefore was no longer a mink and certainly not prey. On the other hand, its death was connected with the trap, and the trap was connected with the man. He hated the man, and therefore if was natural to hate the traps and what was in them.

Distastefully, he sank his canines into the loose skin

across the narrow shoulders, drawing his tongue back from the chill flesh. There was no blood, only a sharp increase in the intensity of the death smell. He lifted his nose to the wind before he bent again and cut a slash down each shoulder and flank. Finally, he gripped the skin beneath the belly fur, and with a powerful twist of his head and shoulders, tore out a large, irregular patch. Spitting the fur out, he stalked away, leaving behind a tattered remnant of what once had been a pelt so perfect, so gleaming and so rich that it had made its owner beautiful, even in death.

With the exception of the stretch north of the beaver pond, the trapline was much as it had been. The fisher covered the area twice, searching for the high-hung baits, but it was not until he heard the sharp clank of a chain, distant but distinct, that he swung out on the lake and found the trapper's most recent trail. He moved along it slowly, taking pains to match his steps to the man's oval snowshoe prints. He could not conceive why the trapper had changed the trail he had followed since the first snow, even though he noticed an interweaving mass of fox tracks on the drifted ice, paralleling the shore. Only when he came upon a newly trapped fox did he begin to understand that part of the trapline had been relocated.

It was a large, red dog fox from somewhere west of the lake. The fisher watched his struggles for a while, but the fox was too angry, too full of fight to attack at the moment. He backtracked the furrow of the clog and discovered it had been buried beneath the snow exactly where another fox had previously marked the trail. The newcomer, placing his paws almost directly in the marks left by the other, had been trapped in mid-stride.

The fisher worked very slowly around the southern swing of the trapline, for now he was inspecting every set closely, rather than only those with living animals in them. Already the brutal cold was being felt. Hour by hour it poured down on the lake, vicious and lethal. More and more, the fisher found animals in the traps either dead or so numb they barely had strength to lift their heads at his approach. One by one, he attacked them, leaving in his wake a trail of destruction. He killed and tore without viciousness, but with a deep determination to destroy everything connected with the trapper. The animals he killed ceased to be real animals. By his own understanding, an animal was capable of flight, and with flight came the hunting chase, the stimulus that raised the killing urge to its natural, perfect pitch. These animals were pinned to one spot.

The freeze continued, becoming harsher and more agonizing every day. The sun rose each morning, offering a promise of warmth it could not fulfill. By the middle of January the fisher knew every trap and set along the section of the line passing through his hunting grounds. It became a silent battleground upon which he and the trapper waged a constant war. As antagonists, they were remarkably well matched. The trapper had his human brain, experience, and skill in his trade. Against these, the fisher pitted his natural intelligence and wiliness, both highly developed qualities in his kind, plus his exceptional agility and incredibly delicate senses. In truth, it was the trapper who held the edge. But the fisher had luck, and a silent ally in the old Ojibway.

The old man did nothing against the trapper directly. His major contribution was to take a walk to the ridge after every fall of snow, no matter how light. Even on the very windy days, when no new snow had fallen, but the old had drifted, he plodded through the cold, obliterating the fisher's homeward tracks with the diamonds of his snowshoes. It was a small thing to do, taking little time and effort, but it seemed to work, for as the weeks dragged on, the trapper failed to locate the den, despite an exhaustive search of the entire southern loop of the trapline.

January was an extremely busy month for the man. He was trapping heavily for fox, anxious to take as many as possible before their fur became too badly rubbed from chasing rabbits and mice through the underbrush. Day by day, the cold forced the luxuriously furred predators to filter into the richer hunting grounds beside the lake. His take increased steadily, but so did the tally of tattered pelts. Finally, he was compelled to take the time, and the traps, to go after the fisher again. His first attempt was very nearly a success.

The set was cleverly conceived. After almost half a day of tracking, he located a gap between the bushes where the fisher habitually passed to reach the marsh. With extreme care, he lifted five patches of crust with his birchwood paddle, three along the line of the fisher's tracks, and two a foot and a half to either side. The central traps were stapled to a heavy deadfall buried beside the trail. The two outlying traps he stapled to chunks of birch, hidden in the drifts beneath the bushes. Then, he painstakingly slid the thin patches of crust back over the gaping jaws. He was quite confident of success.

That night, the fisher padded straight toward the marsh, but as he neared the break in the bushes, he caught sight of a snowshoe print where there had been none the day before. Though the man had covered his tracks for thirty feet around the traps, the fisher was instantly suspicious. He stopped beside a clump of scaly leatherleaf, staring down the passageway, but all he could see were his own paw prints from the previous evening. As he slowly started forward, a snowshoe rabbit crouched beneath the leatherleaf exploded away. The fisher had a vague impression of a dim shape flashing down the trail. He heard the sickening crunch of a trap and high, wavering scream. The scream rose to a peak of unbelievable intensity as a second trap triggered. Then all was silence as the third trap tripped. The fisher swung about and picked his way out and onto the ice through a second gap, forty yards to the east.

When the trapper found the shattered rabbit carcass he swore violently and flung it away. He reset two traps and carried the others to the spot where the fisher had left the woods. There were three separate entries to the ice at this point, framed by two cedars and a pair of low, evergreen sheep laurel shrubs. The fisher's trail led through the central gap, and here the trapper made his set, placing the traps in a blunt arrowhead, with the point toward the opening. As an added measure, he rubbed the metal with cedar, then taking his belt ax, he half severed the lower branches of the cedars and cracked them sharply down to block the other passageways. Finally, after brushing over the set to hide any traces, he obliterated his tracks for sixty feet around.

It was well after midnight when the fisher approached the set. Skirting the spot where the rabbit had died, he moved straight to the trail between the laurels. He was a bare four feet away from the opening before the pungent smell of the freshly cut cedars pentrated his consciousness and stopped him in his tracks.

Warily, he backed away, swung sharply off the trail, and edged forward toward the right-hand tree. He thought he could detect, very faintly, the scent of the trapper, but the strong tansy aroma of the resin was too intense for him to be sure. Crouched, nose to the ground, he began an inspection of the smooth snow between the damaged tree and his original track. He noticed a sharp increase in the cedar scent two feet to the side of the gap and stopped briefly, wondering vaguely why it came from underneath the snow. Finally, he decided it was strange, but not dangerous. He failed entirely to catch the underlying tang of steel as he eased across the spot, his body low to the ground. His forepaw missed the trap by a good foot, but his hind leg dropped directly over the jaws as he shifted his weight back for the final step through the laurels.

He sensed the trap a fraction of a second before it tripped, and it was only his remarkable reflexes and the blind luck of coming on it from the wrong direction that saved him. The moment he felt the hard roundness beneath his foot give slightly, his reflexes sprang into action. He heard the vicious snick as the teeth of the trap gnashed together. A stab of pain lashed through his paw, and for a second he thought he had been trapped again. He fought down the impulse to lunge away, standing frozen until he felt the pain taper off to a sharp, localized burning. The trap was hanging loosely from his leg, the cruel teeth clamped firmly to a single tuft of fur. He shook it impatiently, grunting as the fiber tore loose and the heavy trap dropped to the snow, leaving behind a tender, pink patch of bare skin. He snorted angrily and eased back to the cedar, then sprang into the branches and leaped out the other side to the ice of the marsh.

For another week, the trapper tried to take the fisher in a few, random sets laid along the trails marked by his big, three-inch paw prints. He failed utterly. He caught rabbit and ermine and fox, but the fisher was like smoke on the wind. Nightly, it seemed, he grew more adept at detecting danger. Soon, he even ceased to bother inspecting the man's painstaking work. At the first suspicious sign, he simply took to the trees and bypassed the doubtful spot. Meanwhile, he continued his nightly depredations along the trapline, killing what he wished to eat, destroying what he did not.

The brutal cold continued, and soon its ravages began to show in a marked decrease in the quality of the fox pelts. In a way, the trapper was not too sorry, for he had always found concentrating on one animal boring, with only a few basic set designs to challenge his ingenuity. Furthermore, he felt he could go after the fisher in earnest now. Already, he calculated, the fisher had cost him nearly a fifth of his season's catch, and if the creature continued at the rate he had maintained since Christmas, there was a chance he could damage as much as a quarter of the total winter take. Still, he considered himself lucky the fisher was confining himself to the southern half of the line. He decided to end the month in an all-out effort, by using the equipment pulled from the fox line to triple trap every set within a half day's trek of his cabin.

An hour after coming down from the ridge, the fisher was aware the man had changed tactics. And though he was slowed down, the hidden traps did not interfere with his hunting. He had become quite expert at detecting the scent of steel and so alert to any incongruity that he was able to sidestep all the man's tricks. The trapper rubbed the steel with spruce needles. The fisher knew the spruce smell belonged above the snow, not beneath it. The trapper dabbed the traps with fox dung. The fisher was interested, but considered the smell of fox dung where there were no fox tracks to be suspect. The man even attempted bacon fat. The fisher was revolted. Finally, he tried to lure the fisher with a concoction of the anal glands of mink, steeped for a week in stale ermine urine, and mixed with rancid fish oil. The fisher refused to come within twenty feet of the set.

When the man discovered that the fisher had developed the trick of entering the sets by the same path as the animal that had been caught, he decreased the sensitivity of several traps with thin, whittled willow sticks doubled beneath the pans. Theoretically, the trap would hold under an ermine, but trip under the fisher's greater weight. A month before, it might have worked, but by the time the trapper tried it, the fisher was so finely attuned to every subtlety of the trapline that at the first touch of his paw to the round, hard pan, he jerked back so swiftly the trap failed to trigger. That night, he added a new dimension to his raids as he forsook the ground and learned to drop safely into the cubby sets from above.

By the beginning of February, the trapper was forced to admit the fisher had won the second round of their battle. Two days before, he had discovered that the animal had taught himself the ultimate strategy in evading the traps. During a swift swing through the south section of the line, he had found every trap lying exposed on the snow. The signs showed only too clearly that the fisher had learned to seek out not the traps, but the clogs, dig till he found the stapled chain, and tug it gently until the trap burst clear of the crust. The trapper made one final effort. He placed a trap on the buried clog to which another trap was stapled. The next day he saw, not unexpectedly, that the fisher had simply cleared the chain of the first and flipped it out of the way before going after the second.

When the trapper took stock, he was jolted to find how drastically his catch had fallen off in the previous fortnight. The time he was taking and the traps he was tying up in his efforts to stop the fisher were losing him more pelts than the fisher was likely to destroy. Economically, it was unrealistic to continue after the animal. So with a growing sense of frustration, he returned to his normal routine. He was intensely annoyed, of course, when each day brought more mutilated pelts. In fact, he was disturbed at the depth of his own feelings. Hitherto, he seldom if ever had thought about the animals he tried to kill. He found it quite degrading to realize he was feeling an active hate toward one of them.

Strangely, in all that time, the fisher saw the trapper only once. Dawn, coming a minute or more earlier every day, had caught the fisher still ranging the westerly leg of the trapline. He was padding home, just out of sight of the spring-fed pond, when he heard the sound of wood on wood and the deep rumble of the trapper clearing sleep from his throat. Immediately alert, he leaped straight for the nearest pine, flowed gracefully through the woods, and perched forty feet from the old cabin. He tensed when the trapper appeared with his rifle, but relaxed when he saw the man kick into his snowshoes and stalk toward the beaver pond.

The fisher waited twenty minutes before approaching the cabin. Cautiously, he pushed the door, but it was firmly latched. He made a swift circuit around the building, then slipped up on the woodpile and leaped to the roof. Barring the chimney, there was no apparent way he could enter the cabin. As he dropped down to the ground, the meat locker caught his eye. Built waist high, of split two-inch poles nailed to a heavy frame of two-by-fours, and with light snare wire basket-woven through the corners, it was strong enough to stand up to a starving bear. But not to the fisher. He sprang to the top, sniffed the heavy wrought iron hasp bolted to the side, and hooked his claws into a crack. He heaved, and the hinged half of the top moved, then held. He peered at the short length of snare wire anchoring the pin holding the hasp closed and tugged it curiously. The pin wiggled. It was all the hint the fisher needed. Five minutes later, and the top was open. The fisher reached down and raked back the protective layer of papery birch bark, trying to understand the meaning of the hoard of frozen deer and rabbit meat, and of the strangely stiff and ancient fish. He lowered himself inside, wondering vaguely if this were some sort of den, but the smell of the man was everywhere, underlying the dead meat and fish aromas. He sat on the frigid meat for a moment, trying to think of what to do, but when nothing concrete came to mind, he simply snorted, then urinated on the meat.

When the trapper returned to see the fisher's tracks, the open locker, and the meat frozen into chunks by suspiciously yellow ice, he swore. Then he had the good grace to laugh.

16

DESPITE his preoccupation with the trapper, the fisher did not forget the old man. And after the first, intense period along the trapline, he found himself repairing every few nights to the safer solitudes of the old Ojibway's side of the lake. Almost invariably, he found an egg waiting at the Indian's cabin. Yet, never once did he actually see the old man.

It took a cataclysm of nature to bring them together again.

It was a true arctic blizzard, born above the huge and featureless face of Hudson Bay—one of the far northern storms, which, by a rare combination of circumstances, comes raging south of the tree line. It gave little warning, and only to those living close to nature.

The sun set strangely the evening of the storm. All day long the vaulting cupola of cloud had masked its face, transfusing the light until it took on an underwater quality, pellucid and shadowless and soft as wool. At sunset, just as the fisher came out on his ledge, the clouds drew back from the horizon, revealing a slash of cool, canyon blue, into which the sun slumped, filling the air with a brooding saffron haze. The blizzard hit a half hour later.

The fisher was out on the marsh at the time, carefully investigating the traps camouflaged in the tops of the muskrat push-ups, and the residual light was barely enough to show him which traps held prey and which were still unsprung. Then, in an instant, even that was gone, wiped out by a swirling gust of wind that sliced down across the lake, stinging his eyes with a blast of tiny, ice-hard flakes. He blinked in surprise at the sudden shrinking of his visible world. Now his vision ended in an impenetrable wall an inch from his nose. He could not even see the wall as individual flakes, for their whiteness was lost in the dense blackness they created. For two, nearly three minutes, the wind and snow danced around him; then, swiftly as it had come, the snow squall died. Moments later the blizzard wrapped him in its full fury. Lost in a reeling world of snow, he began to work his way back toward his den. He knew instinctively that for the time being hunting was out of the question.

In all, the blizzard lasted just under four days. It killed nearly half the life around the lake. The toll of insects was immense, for the sleet drove into every crevice, wrapping the dormant bodies in a hyaline shroud, freezing the fluid in their cells, and blanking off the minute supplies of oxygen their hybernating bodies needed. Even the carpenter ants found no escape, for where they burrowed the limbs were weakened, torn off by the wind and strewn on the snow, exposing the frosted black clumps of sleeping ants to the probing ice. The sleet snaked into the tiny entrance holes of engraver beetles and longicorns and the metallic woodborers, and crept silently toward the hibernating larvae and adults. And yet, so slow were the vital life processes of these little creatures, so slight were their demands for warmth and air, that come the spring, many would still be alive. But it would be several years before the birds found this a land of summer plenty once again.

It was the resident birds that suffered most. The black-capped and the boreal chickadees crouched shivering wherever they could find shelter, while hour by hour the internal heat of their bodies drained away, no matter how they ruffed out their feathers. The weeks of extreme cold had depleted their reserves of energy, and now, with the storm cutting off any chance of finding food, all they could do was wait until the strength to grasp their perches flowed out of their feet.

The larger birds fared somewhat better. The huge snowy owl withdrew to the shelter of the spruces and, bundled warmly in the superb cloak of feathers covering him even to his toes, was almost comfortable. But the great gray owl that lived in a hawk's nest to the west of the ridge had his wings frozen to his back, and fell to the ground. He was still alive when the sky cleared, but could do no more than glare at the starving fox that came slipping over the icy crust toward him. To the north, a barred owl forced his way into the upper part of an old ant nest in a dead tamarack and was startled to find two terrified flying squirrels huddled in the narrow bottom of the hole. Surprisingly, he made no effort to attack them during the long, dark hours of their mutual imprisonment.

The gyrfalcon lived, but only because he had felt the blizzard coming and fled southwestward before it hit. He returned to the lake, tired, but well-fed, the following week. The spruce grouse, stupid though they were, sought the densest part of the forest and so survived. But several of the willow ptarmigans, plunging headfirst into the warm protection of the drifts, found themselves locked within glassy coffins, trapped beneath sheets of ice that cut them off from the air and slowly smothered them.

Among the mammals, the rabbits and the shrews felt the blizzard most. Not being burrow builders, the rabbits huddled miserably, their muzzles rimed with hoar frost and eyes tightly shuttered while the tearing wind drained their warmth. Then the sleet came, and they began to die, unable to stand the heat drain flooding out through wet, matted coats. In the last hours of the blizzard, tens of hundreds died. As for the tiny, ferocious shrews, nearly the entire population in the surrounding woods was wiped out. Unable to hunt in the storm, yet still needing up to three times their own body weight in food every day just to keep alive, they swiftly starved to death. Those that survived only did so at the expense of their less cannibalistic brothers.

Deaths among the larger animals were largely accidental. A young doe, lost and wandering out on the lake, fell and shattered a femur. The sleet cloaked her dead body within an hour. Her flesh would remain quite fresh until the spring breakup came, when she would slowly sink to become food for generations of minute aquatic creatures. Three miles to the east, a young buck slipped while picking his way blindly along a rise, breaking a leg as the doe had done. But he died much more swiftly, for the wolves found him and tore out his throat. His body gave them the sustenance to see the blizzard through.

To the fisher, the blizzard brought four of the most uncomfortable days he had ever known. Time and again he pushed through the entrance of his den, hoping the storm would lift enough to let him forage. By the end of the second day, he fought his way up to the ridge, but before he reached the shattered pine, he turned back. Even had he been able to see enough to hunt, he knew the chances of finding any other animal out in the storm were infinitesimal. But by the end of another day, he knew that, regardless of the weather, he was going to have to do something about his hunger, and soon. It was close to four days since he had eaten. The pangs grinding so sharply in the pit of his stomach had dulled to an alarming, tiring ache. He felt an unpleasant lassitude spreading to his limbs, sapping his vitality. Without willing it, he retired into a somnolent, almost hypnotic state, to help his body conserve its dwindling stores of energy.

When he awoke it was to the instinctive, but certain knowledge that his body was on its last reserves. His slender shape held no stores of fat to support him in times of stress. Soon, he would be burning muscle tissue to fight the cold. He lay staring dully at the wedge of luminous snow marking the entrance of the den. Only slowly, did he realize that the light was brighter than it had been for days and that outside, the howling of the wind was gone.

With a surge of energy he came to his feet and ducked down the tunnel. Only the ring of ice narrowing the entrance kept him from plunging out and over the side of the ledge. Teetering slightly, with his claws clicking on the sheer ice, he edged out into the sunlight.

A gentle lull lay across the lake, and even the birds were silent in this hushed hour after the storm. From the sentinel spruce he heard a faint and musical tinkle as ice-bound needles clattered together with a sweet and distant sound. Still, the fisher's body cried for food, and where his eyes roved they passed over the bright beauty, searching instead for the hint of a moving shadow. But nothing stirred. He eyed the root ladder leading to the ridge with a certain apprehension, for a slick sheen overlay the rock and the twisted, sinewy wood. Experimentally, he stretched to probe the upper curve of the roots with his claws. They caught and held in a minute crevice, and moving gingerly, he started to work his way up the sheer face. He was halfway to the top when his claws slithered free, and he toppled. With an immense wrench of his unwilling muscles, he managed to twist in mid-air. His four feet struck the frozen slope simultaneously, and with a resounding crack and clatter, he went through the surface into the softer snow below.

Grumbling and muttering, he pulled himself out, then whirled away toward the trapline. Soon he knew the line was hopeless. The baits and lure sticks were solidly iced. The sets were surrounded by a crust firm enough to carry a good-sized animal without tripping the traps. And of the three he checked, only one held prey, a rabbit solidly encased beneath a glassy hummock.

Impulsively, he swung away from the trapline toward the eastern shore of the lake. His thoughts were mostly of porcupine, but somewhere behind was the subtly prodding memory that in this direction also lay the old man's chicken run.

He headed straight for the first open riffle above the mouth of the stream. As he swung to cut through the bushes lining the sloping bank, he saw a flash of movement at the precise point where ice and water met. Slowly the fisher's eyes adapted to the violent contrasts of light and shadow, and he recognized the reptilian muzzle of a mink with a flopping fish gripped in its jaws. With a rippling heave, the mink drew itself out on the ice.

The fisher plunged forward. Even as he moved, he knew he should have held his attack till the mink had been lulled by feeding. But his hunger was a goad that prodded him into a wild, unthinking dash down the ice-cloaked snow. The mink lunged violently backward and hit the water with a heavy splash. The fisher, with legs flailing, skidded across the ice and followed. Instantly the mink dropped its prize and dove for the bottom.

The fisher bobbed to the surface, buoyed up by the air trapped in his coat. A sudden flicker from the center of the pool pulled his head around. The fish the mink had dropped was slowly regaining its balance and, with a laborious sculling of its caudal muscles, beginning to dive below the edge of the ice. The fisher swerved somewhat clumsily just as the fish disappeared. With the prospect of a delectable meal apparently within easy reach, he gulped a deep breath and plunged confidently after.

He forced his eyes open, searching the jade gloom for the injured fish. It hung in the twilit water, seemingly only inches in front of his nose. The fisher snapped, but to his own surprise, missed. The fish still hung before him, to all appearances within his grasp. He snapped again. After the third miss, he began to realize that, there beneath the surface, things were distorted, actually farther than they seemed. He saw the fish regaining strength, swimming with increasing speed. Furiously, he kicked out, but with every second, the gap widened. Finally, the fish plunged away, down into the increasing shadows.

The fisher ruddered into a wide turn, but to the limits of his vision, nothing moved. The breath was beginning to feel tight in his lungs, so with a kick of his feet, he pushed toward the surface. The surface was gone. A solid sheet of ice pressed firmly on the water. The fisher's head hit with a dull, cushioned crack. He thrust upward with all his strength, thudding against the ice, but the roof held.

With his heart pounding, he lay pressed against the obstinate ice. He tried to think, but, like his aching body, his brain was caught in the coils of its own oxygen-starved agony. He had a vague impression of movement, and with a tremendous effort of will, forced his mind to note the current tugging at him, bumping him along beneath the rumpled under-surface of the ice face. He kicked against it angrily, shooting down to carom off the bottom. Hopelessly, he began to drift toward the surface. Inevitably, his head thudded against the ice again, but he scarcely felt it. Unable to stand the fire blazing in his chest any longer, he gasped out half his supply of air, staring at the big, silver bubble that jiggled before his nose.

With a last, despairing kick, he lunged against the current. He hit the bottom with a jar, which knocked the last of the air from his lungs. Somewhere in his reeling brain was the knowledge that if he breathed, he would die. He held to that one thought as he rose limply among the beautiful, green shadows toward the ice above. But finally, the black closed in, and barely aware, uncaring now, he breathed. His mind awoke only slowly to the delicious realization that he was breathing air.

The light was strange, a mixture of milk and softly shadowed aquamarine. Not until his head cleared slightly did he understand he was still beneath the ice. He had surfaced in a little grotto carved into the thick ice along the bank and pumped full of moist, fresh air by the rushing water. It was small, just high enough for the fisher to float with his head above water. There, he rested, drinking in the heady air until the poisons were washed from his body.

He hung in the dark water, uneasy in the understanding that to reach the open air meant facing the under-water once again. Almost submissively, he plunged beneath the surface. Without knowing why, drawn only by the feeling that the open riffle lay somewhere ahead, he struck out at a sharp angle to the current.

His lungs began to ache and for a moment he paused, deciding whether to forge ahead or return to the air pocket. But something prodded him on, as if his body knew he must take the gamble or fail. Suddenly, he was through and rocketing half out of the water into the joy of clear air and sunlight. He splashed toward the bank, breathing deep, icy lungfuls of the clean, spruce-scented breeze. With a heave that made his muscles crack, he pulled himself up the sloping snow. He took two full steps before he fell.

He lay startled on the snow, wincing at the cramps knotting his legs. The light breeze drove an unexpected chill into his body. Grunting, he forced himself to his feet and staggered on the slope to the protection of the trees. He was shocked at his own weakness. He stopped beneath the downsweeping spruces, but the air, so much colder than the chill water, was like a goad. A hoary redpoll flicked an immaculate white rump from a tree at the edge of the old Ojibway's clearing. The fisher eyed it hungrily, then looked down across the open ground toward the warm, sheltered pocket near the old man's chimney. He wanted nothing more than to lie down and rest, but the awful chill and the hunger draining his strength would not leave him alone. With his breath steaming, he lurched out and across the clearing.

The impulse was totally unconscious. When he reached the middle of the clearing, the most natural thing in the world seemed to be to walk straight to the cabin door and push his way inside.

17

THE OLD MAN had the Ojibways' inherited talent for rigid facial control, but the sudden entrance of the fisher was enough to raise his eyebrows. The fisher paid the Indian no heed whatsoever. With scarcely a glance, he stumbled across to his familiar place by the old iron stove, and slumped to the floor, his nose between his paws.

The Ojibway sat motionless in his chair. He had pulled his worktable from the corner into the warmth of the fire, and had been working on five birds that he had found on the snow with their wings sleeted solidly to their backs. For an hour he had been gently prising their clumped feathers apart, warming their small bodies, and carefully putting tiny crumbs of hard suet into their gasping mouths, stroking their throats to help them swallow. And at last, the birds were coming to life, balancing precariously on their feet as the concentrated nourishment in the fat was soaked up by their bodies.

The old man was quite shocked by the fisher's appearance. He stepped close to where the animal lay. The fisher lifted his head and studied the Indian's face with his steady gaze. The old man's eyes crinkled. It pleased him to see the animal, even now; behaving with the simple dignity of a natural aristocrat, and he knelt, looking for any signs of physical injury. There were none, and the alertness of the fisher's eyes seemed to rule out disease. The old Ojibway noticed that, though the stove's heat was enough to steam the dampness rising rising from the fisher's coat, the animal still was clenching his teeth against the shivers that wracked his body. Exhausted and damned hungry, thought the old man. Fell in the water too, he muttered to himself as he shrugged into his parka and stepped outside, though he could not conceive why the fisher had stayed in long enough to become so thoroughly drenched.

The fisher stared at the five birds moving gingerly about the work table and for a moment considered going after the big jay. But a strange determination kept him from it, a reluctance born of sensing a vague connection between the birds and the man. Two days ago, he would have overcome his scruples, for then his hunger had been sharp and demanding; now it was dull and enervating.

The old man reappeared, letting in a sudden chill that ruffled the birds' feathers and sent a shudder down the fisher's spine. The Indian rummaged in his parka pockets, and drew out three tan eggs, laying them in a bobbing row well within the animal's reach. One after another, the fisher drew the eggs between his paws, nipped them open, and drank them down. He blinked toward the firelight when he was done, savoring the warm feel of food in his stomach. Then to his surprise, he felt a sharp and unexpected stab of hunger.

His belly gave a huge, tumbling rumble. He gazed

down at it, as the old man chuckled and moved across to the work table. The Indian sliced three bite-sized chunks from the birds' lump of suet and laid them beside the egg shells. The fisher nosed them, then pushed them away. The Indian moved them back. The fisher turned his head away. The old man clucked in gentle reproof, picked up a piece, and extended it toward the fisher on the flat of his palm.

The fisher stared up into the seamed face above him, blinking at the strange feeling that swept over him, a feeling of swift understanding. It was gone as quickly as it came, but it left behind a slender bridge of trust. He acknowledged it by dropping his head, and with a fastidious wrinkling of his lips, picked up the lump of suet, chewed briefly, and swallowed.

It was tastier than he had thought it would be. He ate the three pieces and two more the old man gave him. Soon, he was suspended between two pools of glowing warmth, one from within, and the other from the stove by his side. The old Ojibway waited until the fisher was breathing deeply, then tiptoed to the far corner, tugged the white rabbit blanket free of the few piled furs, and gently spread it about the sleeping form. The fisher muttered drowsily and nuzzled the soft pelts dreamily as he had done that first afternoon, many months ago.

He awoke to the sound of the old Ojibway's soft snores. A sharp, intriguing smell rose from beside him, and he made out a rectangle of birch bark piled with chunks of pale, raw fish and dark, well-hung deer meat. He nipped into the fish immediately, downing it in a dozen bites. He nosed the deer meat away at first, but hunger was still a prod in his stomach, and so he finally tried a piece. He was quite delighted with its tender succulency, so different from the dead meat he had known, the rotten putrescence of carrion, the cold visceral rankness of meat only a day dead, but unbled. Then, with his stomach bulging, he came to his feet in a long, rippling, feline stretch. He studied the old man's face as he slept, crossed to the worktable to inspect the birds, and then padded to the door. With a disapproving sniff at the rack of rifles, he hooked his claws around the edge of the door and eased it open a few inches. It thudded softly behind him as he slipped out.

The air had a friendly crispness and felt almost mild after the weeks of cold and days of storm. He separated each scent and sound distinctly, and as the fisher drew it deeply into his lungs, he knew again the intense pleasure of just being alive. The night was rich with movement, with the scurrying of rabbits, with the swift, soundless sweeps of hunting owls, and the castanet clatter of the deer trying to clear the branches of the sheaths of ice.

He had no exact idea of the time, though his inner clock told him the night was advancing toward dawn. Well-fed and warm, he ambled through the darkness, gradually working his way in the direction of the ridge. There, he lowered his head to study the drop to his den. Even in the faint light he could see the ice still cloaking the rocks and roots. Four times he tried to work his way down, but it was hopeless. The blizzard had spread an inch-thick layer of sleet on the face of the granite, impervious to anything but the brute force of an ax or the mellow coaxing of the sun.

The fisher spent the day sleeping peacefully in one of the empty fox dens north of the Indian's clearing, for though he had gone to the old man's cabin in time of need, he preferred his solitude when need was answered. That night he killed a porcupine whose greed for fallen deer antler held it crouched too long, gnawing a branched piece of bone. He ate heavily of the fragrant flesh. Satisfied, he returned to the fox den hours before dawn.

A sound like hundreds of tiny, muffled chimes awoke the fisher shortly after midday. He stepped outside into a spellbindingly beautiful ice shower from the trees. The heaps of broken crystal lay everywhere, catching the sun and casting it back in a resplendent, prismatic blaze. It was more than the fisher could resist, and for a half hour he cavorted through the clearings, scattering the icy jewels. At last, with his first burst of exuberance spent, he loped toward the ridge. The sun had cleared the ladder, warming the underlying rock and roots until the frozen mantle had peeled away. The fisher swarmed down the twisted roots, kicked the shards of ice from the ledge, and plunged down the tunnel to his den. A quick but thorough investigation showed that no other animal had entered during his days of exile. He sat on the ledge, confirming his proprietorship for a pleasant, sunny hour, then came down the ridge and started for the trapline.

Unknowingly, his attitude toward the trapline had

undergone a change. Originally, he had started his depredations because his hatred of the trapper had translated easily into hatred of everything connected with the man. But as the weeks passed and the memory of the wounds he had suffered at the trapper's hands dimmed, his rage began to abate. The loathing he felt for the man did not lessen, but by the time of the blizzard, he was no longer ranging the line as a compulsive destroyer. Simply put, with the passage of time, the destruction became less vengeful, more habitual. Now when he returned to the line, he did so calmly, finding a simple comfort in the following of a familiar routine. It was well, for where before he had moved with ruthless determination, now he would raid the sets with the skill of a craftsman.

He found no indication of hidden traps near any of the sets along the southern swing of the line. It was barely sunset when he reached the beaver pond. There, against the limpid light, the strangely canted sapling at the near end of the beaver dam stood out like a shout.

The fisher stopped, his ears cocked and his nose straining to separate the scents. Distinct above all others was the smell of freshly cut wood. The tree was a landmark to the fisher; as long as he had lived by the lake it had stood as an anchor to the beaver dam. Now it was down, cut three feet above the roots. The butt of the fallen upper portion was still attached to the stump by a few split fibers, so the sloping trunk formed an angled arch above the trail. He saw the lower branches had been bent sharply back, forming a dense barricade across the end of the dam and leaving only a single, foot-and-a-half-high gap for him to pass through to reach the crest beyond. Suspiciously, he put his head inside the opening. His nose gave him no warning. His eyes took in an odd, thin, circular filament ringing the gap and his head. He inspected it and decided it was a vine. He was just about to step through the barrier, when his eyes moved to the left and down. Partially covered by the toppled crown, but clearly etched in the long, slanting light of evening, was the distinct oval of a snowshoe. The fisher went rigid, then with immense care, backed out of the now-ominous gap.

He might well have forgotten his suspicions had the strange barrier remained untouched, but on the next night, he discovered its deadly purpose. By dying, a young wolf showed it to him. The richly furred form lay hunched queerly against the stump at the end of the dam. The toppled crown of the tree had been wrenched free and cast several feet away. The wolf hung suspended from where his neck had touched the stump, collapsed in a circle of trampled snow. The fisher approached the still form circumspectly, though he knew the rumpled ground made it most unlikely that there would be any hidden traps. He peered at the slender ligature twined round and round the post and into the disordered ruff of the wolf's throat. It was the thing he had taken as a vine, but when he sniffed it, he caught the smell of steel. He could not conceive how this slender cord, which a day ago had given no warning, smelled of the most dangerous scent he knew when wound in overlapping circles around the post. Later that night, when he came across another oddly toppled sapling, he automatically gave it a wide berth.

Throughout the weeks that followed, the new battle raged along the trapline. It was a battle in which each, in his own way, was fighting for survival—the fisher for his life, the man for his profits and his ego. But this time, the contest was less equal. True, it was still the man's wit, his greater physical skill and ingenuity pitted against the fisher's acuteness and his growing knowledge of the ways of the man. But it was a contest that circumstances weighted in favor of the fisher. The trapper could produce only a dozen snares from his limited supply of heavy wire. He had even less light-gauge material for the more complex deadfall and spring-pole snares. But what counted against him most heavily was the hunger of the animals around the lake. After the damage done to the food supplies by the blizzard, the predators and their prey were ravenous enough to go after any bait.

The man was ingenious in deploying his equipment. He used every trick he knew, some of them so complex they were self-defeating. He made several trail and ground-bait sets with a simple trigger mechanism that released a weight suspended from a tree branch above the snare. The falling weight was designed to snap the noose closed and haul the kicking animal off the ground like a felon on a gibbet. But the fisher no longer traveled by well-defined trails on this side of the lake, nor would he touch either baits or scent lures, so the trapper harvested mostly rabbits for his trouble. He built several drop-weight snares in the trees beside trap sets where the fisher occasionally entered from above, but the slender wire, the masterfully carved wooden trigger mechanisms, and above all the hanging weights were ample warning to the fisher.

Each evening the trapper spent hours stretching pelts, cleaning them of fat and flesh with his slender deer-bone scraper, and building in his mind the snare sets he would construct the next day on the trail. It became something of a game with him, and the number of design variations he came up with was quite remarkable.

He built a half dozen different sets in the classic spring-pole pattern, but after a week was forced to abandon them, for he found that the bent saplings, which provided the power to close the noose and jerk the animal free of the ground, quickly lost their resiliency in the cold. He turned to the lifting-pole snare, a large and complex mechanism where a long, slim pole, with a snare at one end and a heavy weight at the other, was balanced like an off-center seesaw across a low tree fork. He quite enjoyed building the big, brutal devices, and tested and adjusted each until the slightest touch to the trigger would send the weighted end of the pole plunging to the snow, while the end with the snare pivoted in a swift arc upward, snapping the noose closed. However, after another week, the trapper was forced to admit he was a victim of his own ingenuity. The tracks showed that the fisher flatly refused to come within thirty feet of the blatantly unnatural construction.

During the final week of February, the trapper went back to traps again, in the somewhat vain hope that time and familiarity might have dulled the fisher's alertness. It was a total waste of effort. Within three days the fisher had discovered every extra clog, dug them out, and left the traps lying openly on the snow. The trapper gathered them up, returned to his cabin, cooked a lonely meal, and sat back to think things out once more.

Past experience made it obvious that to kill the fisher would take a great degree of luck or a great expenditure of time. It would have been quite different had he been able to find the fisher's den. For a while he had suspected the old man of being connected with the fisher's uncanny ability to go to ground. He had even spent an afternoon on the ridge after he had noticed that the old Indian often climbed to the point, but could find no evidence. And so, the trapper had finally concluded the fisher denned across the lake and had given up the search. Which left him with his original problem: he had an animal on his hands that was costing him money, but he knew it would cost him more in time and work to keep after the animal until he killed it. The sensible thing to do, he realized, was simply to concentrate on collecting from the traps before the animal visited them.

Regretfully, he laid aside the figure-4 trigger mechanism he was carving. But he felt a curious unwillingness when he set the delicate pieces down and sheathed his knife, and suddenly realized how much he had enjoyed the past few weeks, how pleasant his evenings had been as he busied himself with the problems of designing and building new snare mechanisms. Looking back, he could see how the challenge had lightened the enervating routine of the mid-winter trapline.

At the same time, he was startled to find that his attitude toward the fisher had undergone a curious change. He remembered his past attitudes—first the annoyance, then the shift to anger, and on its heels the sobering realization that, for the first time, an animal had become more than a thing to him. Following that, there was the frustration as, week by week, the fisher dodged his best efforts, and paralleling it, the dawning comprehension that an animal could be as intelligent on its own ground as a man was on his. And now, after the most pleasurable month he had spent all winter, he was developing a growing, if grudging respect for the fisher.

18

MANIFESTLY, on the surface, winter still held the land, but in myriad hidden places, the faint urgings of spring were being felt. As early as mid-February, the sun-drenched snow around the tree trunks had come alive with dancing springtails, minute and lively insects that littered the frozen crust like a sprinkling of wind-tossed cinders. By the open stretches of the streams, the stone-fly nymphs crawled out into the freezing air, pausing to split their skins and emerge as long-bodied, fully winged adults. Then, running with a rat-like scamper, they struck out among the frost flowers to seek their kind, to mate, and then to return to lay the next generation's eggs in the swift, icy water.

The snow that sifted down from the occasional lowering clouds no longer cut and stung; now it came in huge, woolly eiderdown flakes, satisfyingly heavy with moisture. Every day at noon the sun stood higher in the sky. The snowy owl felt it tug mystically at some buried racial memory. Grudgingly, it left the lake and began a slow journey north to its tundra nesting grounds. The great horned owl found a wandering mate, and together they took over a hawk's nest from which they hunted together. Then, unmindful of snow or cold, impelled by the lengthening hours of daylight that signaled their own personal spring, they mated.

Meanwhile, in the triangle of second-growth timber below the ridge, wherever the snow was thin, the early skunk cabbages felt the growing light and moved into the first, slow stages of germination.

The fisher, too, felt the season change, but the signs meant little to him, for his had always been an autumn and a winter world. He had as yet to experience a land reborn in spring. Still, a chord was struck within, and he reacted to the message, whispered by the southern winds, that every day the earth was tilting more and more toward spring. By March, he found himself coming out earlier, sitting upon his ledge to feel the friendly afternoon sun soak his sleek, dark fur.

He spent fewer hours along the trapline, for the trapper had stopped building snare sets, and the fisher began to lose interest in the line's repetitious routine. He still destroyed pelts, but more and more haphazardly, until the trapper began to feel hopes such as he had not allowed himself all winter. The fisher was using the line as little more than a lunch counter, preferring to spend his hours after feeding in watching the other animals at their uninhibited mating games.

Now, of all the things going on about him, it was the actions of the female that denned somewhere above the northern limit of his hunting ground that intrigued the fisher most.

He had seen her three times in the month following the blizzard. The first was only a few days after the storm. She appeared in the night as a flicker of green eyeshine and a dark and slender shape silhouetted against the snow. He realized she must have been watching and following him. He took out after her, but lost the trail in the unfamiliar territory north of his home range. A week later he saw her standing in the twilight on the banks of the northern stream. Cautiously, he began to close the space that separated them, but at his first step, she dove away, leading him on a wild chase through the trees before she was able to lose him completely.

Several weeks passed before she allowed him to see her again. This time, he found her north of the lake, crouched in the early dusk, devouring a flying squirrel. She paid no attention to him until she had finished, then she stretched, sat back, and looked him over. As he started forward, she moved away, turning to look back meaningfully over her shoulder. She led him steadily north, past his own hunting boundary, to the edge of a small clearing marked by a superb birch that sprouted five graceful trunks from a common root. Then, to his surprise, she turned and snarled at him. He stepped toward her. The snarl rose to a scream, and she crouched, hackles bristling and fangs bared. The fisher took one look into her eyes and saw she meant business. He turned and fled. It was the first fight he had ever run from. For some reason, it seemed the right thing to do.

Back near the clearing the female slipped into a carefully hidden den under an old pine stump. The life she had been carrying within her for almost a year of pregnancy was stirring. In a month to six weeks she would birth a litter, and a few days after, be ready to mate again.

Late in March, the sun set through a sullen sky. The wind made up to a gale, and the month was ushered out in a swirl of dazzling snow. All the next day, winter heaved its expiring sigh through the tall trees and across the wind-scarred wastes of the open lake. Then the gale died, the sun peered through the watery gray clouds, and winter was gone. On the ledge below the ridge, the fisher stepped from his tunnel, lifted his muzzle to the sky, and for a long, luxurious moment, stood bemused by an April blindness.

He looked north and east, where the smoke from the old Ojibway's chimney hung in cottony white puffs above the spruces, like giant dandelions gone to seed. His eyes drifted westward. Everything was as it had been since the first heavy snows had fallen. And yet the sky, the air, the texture of the snow beneath his feet shouted that nothing was the same, that somehow the world stretched out before him was new and utterly different. He inhaled the crisp, spruce-scented air, the virile, earthy smell of early growth. When at last he slipped up on the ridge and turned away to hunt, he carried the wonder with him, not realizing that the great and stirring change he felt was also taking place inside himself.

Meantime, around the lake, all living things—plants, animals and men—waited impatiently for the first spring day.

The old Ojibway greeted the season with his annual sugaring trip to the woods, driving his small stock of metal spiles into the sunny sides of the birches and hanging on them the containers he had fashioned through the winter from birch bark and tamarack roots and spruce gum. The sap was not as thickly sweet as the rich blood of the maples farther south, but he enjoyed its delicate flavor. Or perhaps it was that he enjoyed most the clear, clean, fragrant air after a winter inside his cabin. Often he would stop and listen to the gentle dropping of the sap. One drop a minute or maybe two, twelve thousand drops a gallon, five gallons to be boiled down to a pint of syrup or a ridiculously tiny two ounces of granular, yellow sugar.

He laughed when he thought of it. So much labor for such a small reward, but what joy there was in the laboring, for while he stood listening, he could journey with his eyes and experience firsthand the signals of the young year's rebirth: the greening of the birch twigs that drove the hungry deer into ecstasies of eating, the gradual evaporation of the hard-packed snow until the drifts took on the look of shining mounds of granulated sugar, sprinkled with a peppery grit of bouncing springtails. He saw the bud scales push forth impatiently from underneath the bundle scars of bilberries, laurels, and the graceful scrub willows and alders, bursting into early growth in such fantastic numbers that steady pruning by the ravenous rabbits left scarcely a mark.

He saw too, in the few places where the lake ice was faintly transparent, the dead and dying fish, doomed creatures that with the spring breakup only weeks away had lost their yearly battle against creeping suffocation. Like many men who live very close to the essentials of life, the old Ojibway hated death, while recognizing both its need and its inevitability. But this form of death, pointless and unselective, depressed him most.

In unwitting compensation, he let his thoughts drift to the great surge of births he knew were taking place even now within the dens of the animals. It was a spectacle that delighted him, and he took the time, this as every year, to seek out the hidden places where the mothers brooded the young they had carried throughout so many harsh, demanding months. He saw the minute, newly born rabbits nuzzling frightened mothers that had plucked their breasts bare of fur to line the nest for the young. Once, while the big fox was away hunting for his new family, the old man tracked down the burrow just north of his cabin, and smiled benignly at the snarling, silver vixen protecting six blind, dark-furred bundles with gleaming, white-tipped tails. He watched a slim ermine carrying mice to a narrow den where his mate nursed the eight incredibly tiny, flesh-colored kittens she had carried for nearly ten months. During the next few days, he saw the male hunting incessantly, driven to enormous effort by his mate's need to supply the milk for a brood that demanded half their own weight in nourishment every day.

Not all were devoted parents. The male pine martens carried on their carefree existence with no thought for the females they had mated nine months before.

None approached the log and tree nests where the females brooded fondly over two to four one-ounce, down-covered kittens. The females accepted the responsibility and would honor it with great devotion until autumn. Only then, after months of careful instruction, would they turn their young away to fend for themselves while their bodies labored to create new litters from late-summer matings with other capricious males. The male lynx were equally remiss, but they had little choice. Any male foolish enough to enter the den where the female he had mated was nursing her kittens would be attacked. The Indian chuckled at the thought, for it brought the young fisher to mind. This was the mating time, and from what the old man knew of fisher behavior, the young animal, if he found a mate, was in for quite an experience.

The fisher, in truth, was not enjoying himself at all. He was troubled, and what was most upsetting, could not understand why. A barely perceptible yearning had begun to grow inside him. At first the yearning came spasmodically, welling up swiftly, then fading back. Yet it grew more insistent every day, until he found himself wandering late each night, returning to his den unwillingly, feeling oddly unsatisfied.

During the first days of the month, his tempers fluctuated with the ebb and flow of the alien hunger within. When it clamored inside him, he stalked the trapline in an ugly mood. Had he been an older animal, he might have adapted to the pressures, but this was his first year, and he had no seasoning to draw upon to guide him through the glandular upheaval taking place. And so, he reacted by extremes, one moment the sadistic killer, the next a blatantly benign creature that romped alone, playing mysterious, meaningful games with the comic concentration of a kitten. But these peculiar vacillations only marked the first stage of his slow, painful trip to sexual maturity, for all at once, he became subdued and introspective, spending hours each afternoon and evening sitting on his ledge or high in the old, sentinel spruce, gazing toward the north.

19

Toward the middle of the month it snowed. It was the last snowfall of winter, and it was a thing of rare beauty, the perfect snowfall that comes but once in a dozen years. At midnight the snow began, silencing the woods, hushing the hunting shrieks of weasels. The flakes were huge and woolly, like drifting feathers from the breasts of birds or captive bits of cloud. They came straight down, clinging where they touched.

The fisher wandered aimlessly, snorting at the tickle of a giant flake on his nose or shaking away the white wig that settled between his ears when he sat too long, staring northward. After a few days of surcease, the hunger had crashed back on him until it was a yammering in his loins. Still he could not discover what the hunger was, only that it was a hunger beyond the hunger of the belly.

He crossed the open lake to the old Ojibway's cabin, found a snow-crowned egg upon the woodpile, and ate it, crushing the shell with a swat of his paw when it was done. Finally, finding no release in a familiar pattern, he slumped back to his den.

He dozed fitfully through the dawn, held at the uncomfortable edge of awareness by the tensions within. Muttering furiously to himself, he slouched outside. It was barely midmorning. The lack of sleep had put him in vicious temper. With a rumble in his throat, he sprang up on the ridge and headed in a stiff-legged, angry trot for the trapline.

He created more havoc in the next few hours than he had in the previous two weeks, for the trapline was heavy with booty captured during the snowfall. He cut a swath across the southern leg of the line, killing in succession a fox, an ermine, and a marten, all female, all out scavenging food for litters now slowly dying in their nests. He ripped the pelts brutally, more violently each time. Reaching the marsh, he raged after a grizzled old muskrat plodding through the misty air on his annual courting trip and stomped for several minutes around the icy escape hole where the muskrat had plunged to escape. Cutting back through the woods toward the beaver pond, he sought some relief in meticulously digging through several sets, leaving the traps scattered openly beneath the sky. Fifty feet in from the northerly stream a mink lay trapped in a cubby. He killed her in one lightning strike and viciously ruined the gleaming pelt. He followed her trail back to the hole beneath a streamside juniper where he could hear the muffled whimperings of her swiftly starving kittens. But it was too small to enter, and so he stalked away along the stream.

A hundred yards north he stopped as if struck. Near the streamside, among a patch of snowberry vines wreathing a weathered spur of rock, he caught a distinct and delicious pungency. With every muscle tense, he dropped his head toward the frost-fractured stone and inhaled deeply. A wondrously spermatic musk hung there. It swirled through his lungs and burst into his brain. With an ecstatic yelp, he raced north and west toward the clearing with the graceful birch, knowing at last that beneath the five stately trunks lay what he had been seeking. He covered the mile in a matter of minutes. When he burst through the underbrush he found her waiting, almost as if she had been expecting him.

Now that he had arrived, the fisher had no idea what he was supposed to do. Instinct had brought him here, and instinct would lead him surely through the patterns of the mating act, but not till the inner trigger was tripped. Fortunately the female, mature in her six or seven winters, knew exactly what was needed. She strode forward and sat in the middle of the clearing, looking everywhere but at him. He started toward her cautiously. She waited until he was within reach, then with a scream, walloped him. He scarcely realized that she had been careful not to use her claws when she had struck. Oddly enough, he had neither the desire to fight nor to defend himself. He was quite happy to take anything she offered.

Had he been able to comprehend beauty, he would have thought her glowing sleekness beautiful. She was a striking animal, a lithe and graceful creature with a superlatively dark coat and huge, liquid eyes set within a perfectly proportioned triangular head. Across the crown and edging each gently rounded ear, a faintly grizzled cap of fur formed a nimbus about her sensitive face. To the fisher, she was an object of incredible desire, and even now, at their first real meeting, he could sense a feeling of protectiveness toward her.

She slipped across the clearing to her den beneath the old stump and slid partly into the carefully camouflaged entrance tunnel to check her newborn young. Content, she backed out, meticulously replacing the screen of dried grass that helped protect her kits from the chill while it filtered the faint light reaching their birth-shuttered eyes. Then she turned to the fisher with a bubbling, musical chuckle.

He started forward. She screamed and raced for the trees. The fisher found himself bellowing a hideous, happy shriek and tearing through the trees in pursuit. The female matched him scream for scream until the rollicking chase became a contest of speed and daring and concentrated lung power. He was bigger than she, and considerably more powerful; time after time in the frantic, giddy race through the treetops he nearly had her in his grasp. But she knew the territory as he knew his home to the south, and where he paused to gauge a leap, she sprang sure-footed into space. Still, he had cut her lead to scarcely a yard by the time they made a great circle back to the clearing beneath the birches where, as of one accord, they collapsed panting in the snow.

Abruptly, the fisher trotted over to where she lay, and with a swift twist of his forepaw flipped her on her back. She blinked up at him calmly, panting slightly, her four legs relaxed in the air, while he inspected her critically. He inhaled the pleasant muskiness of the fur in the warm hollow of her throat, sniffed the memory-invoking milkiness around her four mammae, still quite small in these early days while her kittens needed barely a quarter ounce of milk a day, and finally caught the fruitful fragrance of her soft, tumescent vulva. And again the unsuspected synapses clicked in his brain, telling him that he had found another part of what he did not know he had been searching for.

With a fluid ripple of muscle she came to her feet, touched his nose very gently with her own, then turned half away, glancing over her shoulder at him. Clumsily, he gripped the loose skin across her shoulders and inexpertly threw a foreleg over her back. She grumbled and slipped out from his hold, cooing softly in her throat. Again, he tried to mount her, but the second effort was more awkward than the first. He ended with one paw across her haunches, standing at almost a full forty-five degree angle to her flank. The female snorted her disgust, wrenched away, and stamped into her den.

The fisher paced anxiously in front of the burrow, making the little cooings and chucklings in his throat he had heard her make, but the only answer was an occasional surly grunt from the dark tunnel. Finally, he gave up and stretched out on the moist snow. After about a half hour she came out, stalking determinedly toward him. He rose to touch noses as she reached him, but received instead a sharp nip on the flank. She stumped a few feet away. Timorously, he started toward her. She moved like lightning, and this time, got him by the ear, nipping it hard enough to puncture the cartilage. He yelped sharply and jerked away.

Then, for the first time, he lost his temper and did

precisely what instinct directed. With a piercing hiss, he lunged for her, leaping on her back and burying his teeth in the fur and skin of her shoulders. Unbidden, his forelegs clamped down around her rib cage in an iron grip. A force from beyond himself suddenly grasped his haunches and drove them forward. He had a fleeting impression of softness and warmth, and then all rage was swept away by a great tide of sensation that surged through him in mounting waves. He was aware of nothing else for nearly two hours.

She was barely panting when he finished. He was gasping, but he blinked and snorted his happy devotion while she pranced a few playful steps upon the snow before disappearing to feed her young. The fisher squinted at the late afternoon sun. Ordinarily he had an excellent time sense, but during the long, rhythmical moments of mating it had deserted him completely. He slipped up to the crown of a slender pine, drawing the air into his lungs and listening with a reawakened ear to the birds. He felt deeply peaceful, content to lie upon the bough and let the sights and sounds and scents wash around him. Then, with the first, early star, he became alert to the sound he had unconsciously been waiting for. The female was below the tree, cooing softly for him to come down.

Their second embrace lasted more than three hours. This time, their joining was less precipitant and moved with surprising symmetry. Both were superbly coordinated, beautifully muscled animals and fell into a natural rhythm in which each movement by one brought a counterplaying movement by the other. Finally, he dropped away from the female, and casually turned toward the den. He scarcely saw the black flash of her movement, but suddenly she was blocking his way, fangs bared and ready. The fisher made no attempt to face her down. As she slipped into the entrance, he turned and skinned up into the crotch of a large birch trunk. He dozed till nearly midnight, when the dove-like coo of her voice called him down. This time the mating lasted an hour and a quarter. He did not know if she called again that night, for he was overcome by fatigue.

Morning found her waiting impatiently in the clearing. He gazed at her and danced about her before he darted forward. Refreshed by sleep, unflagging, this time they remained joined for three hours. When they were done, she nipped playfully at his flank and darted back to her kittens.

A flash of movement caught the fisher's eye, and he turned to see a deer mouse shaking the moisture from his hind legs before a flooded tunnel. Suddenly the mouse saw the fisher, stiffened, and fled. The fisher padded across to the tiny opening, and when a second mouse darted out, killed it cleanly. He bent to nip the little morsel down, but picked it up instead, and trotted toward the den, cooing plaintively. The female popped her head out, and when he dropped his gift, slipped forward to inspect it. He eased toward the den and managed to push halfway inside the tunnel before she noticed what he was about. He heard her snarl and stopped, but before he could back out, she had her claws in his flank. Her strength surprised him and he dodged away, blinking when she whuffed a further warning.

Shortly after noon he saw his mate amble from the tunnel and stretch luxuriantly. He dodged around to a limb on the far side of the trunk when she started along the margin of the trees, calling with her unique, inviting chuckle. He waited until she was directly beneath and sprang, rocketing straight down the trunk. As she jerked around, he dodged between the trees in a riotous zigzag. She raced after, the snow flying in clumps from her paws. A deadfall loomed before him and he flashed around it and skidded to a stop. When she shot past he screeched and charged, catching her off balance. He pranced around her, then leaped forward, and gripped her by the shoulders. It took a moment for her to realize what he was about, but his weight on her back triggered a swift response.

Inevitably, she went straight back to her young, but within a half hour she was out again, calling him to follow as she trotted northward. He loped on her heels as she combed back and forth through the woods, leading him along trails only she could see. Twice they passed the trapper's sets. She became exceedingly anxious when he insisted on inspecting them. After that, she moved toward an area where the trapline did not run. Within an hour, they found a porcupine. Twice she started for it, but each time the fisher blocked her way, pushing her back toward the shelter of a bilberry. When finally she agreed to stay out of harm's way, he made the kill. He dragged it to where his mate sat, then stood back to offer her first choice of the tender meat. After a while he joined her, and they crouched side by side, shoulders touching and heads intimately together.

Later in the afternoon, he found an opportunity to enter the forbidden burrow. Just before sunset, she left the den to relieve herself, trotting fastidiously into the woods. The fisher saw his chance and was at the tunnel within seconds. It was extremely dim inside, but filled with the warm enchantment of milk and musk and dried grass and earth. He nosed the screen of fragrant grasses aside and ducked into the warm hollow.

The cavity beneath the roots was lined around the sides and an inch deep on the floor with a crinkly, interwoven mass of sedge and dried fern and leaves, while around the bottom was an edging of fur the female fisher had pulled from assorted kills and from her own magnificent coat. In a squirming lump against the wall were four kittens. The tiny, slate-colored creatures enchanted the fisher, and he stretched out beside them, inhaling their bland, sweet odor and blinking delightedly when the largest of the four put out an enormous paw—enormous in relation to the rest of him—and whacked the fisher blindly on the nose. He rolled happily on his back, snorting at the tickle of the minute claws when they began to climb on his chest.

Abruptly, he heard the female's angry snarl and the rattle of her claws as she came scrabbling down the tunnel. Her face was a mask of rage when she shot her head into the burrow, but she calmed quickly when she saw him lying blissfully spread-eagled on his back, with two kittens rooting at his chest and one creeping adventurously along each arm. Still, she made it clear that he was trespassing, by backing out of the entrance and grunting insistently. She cuffed him as he passed, but it was tolerantly done. Her claws barely nicked his ear.

He slept through the afternoon and early evening, awakening again to her demanding croon. They mated until midnight, then he wandered alone for a few hours, savoring the rich, spermatic scent of earth released at last from snow and ice. He killed an unlucky rabbit and carried it back to the den. They shared it, and then they mated once again.

He felt a change in her the next day, a transient but perceptible withdrawal that faded the moment he mounted her. After an hour, she pulled away and ducked into the den, flatly refusing to let him either precede or follow her. She paid no attention to his wistful croonings, even refusing a spruce grouse he killed. He wandered disconsolately around the clearing, muttering to himself, then returned to call her from the den. After nearly an hour of urging, she came outside. He mounted her with practiced ease, but found her disturbingly unresponsive. After three-quarters of an hour she pulled away. When he tried to mount her again she snarled and wrenched out from beneath him. Refusing to be deterred, he started toward the den, but she was on him like a flash, slashing two hard, purposeful blows to his head. He leaned forward to touch her nose and she bit him—hard. With a last, harsh hiss, she turned and slid out of sight.

For most of that evening, he trotted back and forth before the burrow, crooning and whimpering plaintively to her. Her answer was a stream of muffled snarls. Bewildered, and not a little indignant, he finally stalked away and slowly climbed the birch.

The night sounds wrapped him round, and gradually he began to listen, more intent and more alert to their messages than he had been for days. He yawned toward the moon and began to groom his fur. In working down his flanks, he noted vaguely that his testicles were no longer swollen. Slowly, it was borne to him that all the tensions, all the inward pressures that had made the last weeks so black were gone. He felt a great calm within, a reawakened interest in the world around him and, almost incidentally, a definite dimming of his interest in the female. Suddenly, he was swept by the desire to return to the lake, to the delight of the old Ojibway's eggs, and to his own warm den, filled with his own personal smells. He dropped from the birch and left the clearing without even giving his mate's den a farewell sniff.

20

For the trapper the season was nearly over. He had begun to pull up stakes in preparation for the spring breakup. He still had traps out for those animals on which the season had not yet closed, and, of course, he was still trapping fox, on which the season never ended. But the special sets for lynx, for marten, mink, and otter he was forced to dismantle. He did so grudgingly, for though he had reached his quota on lynx peltries, he was still below limit on the others. Especially marten. His being under quota had been almost exclusively the fisher's work.

The trapper considered himself an essentially honest man. Thus, he had not felt he was breaking the law, so much as bending it, in the way he had distributed his remaining traps. There was no closed season on ermine, and if the ermine cubbies he set up happened to attract a few pine marten, he would take it as the blind working of a friendly fate. Similarly, if the muskrat sets should catch a mink or the beaver sets waylay an otter, he would accept in good grace, up to his quota.

In truth, he had known he was risking his license by playing fast and loose with the regulations, but he counted on the lake's isolation to see him through. Besides, he had argued with himself, after a winter spent with that damned fisher in the area, he deserved a little extra time to balance out. And there was always the chance one of the fox sets might pick off the fisher.

But now the picture had changed, and he could not leave the fisher to chance.

The trapper reached for his pipe, thought better of it, and snapped a twig from the willows surrounding him. He chewed it thoughtfully, hardly aware of the reborn resiliency of the sappy wood. He spat on the sugary snow, scratched his beard with the frayed end of the twig, and hunkered himself into a more comfortable position.

This was the second night he had crouched here near the water's edge, screened by the willows, staring through gritty eyes toward the old man's clearing, waiting for the slim, black form he knew must inevitably come. He was growing anxious now, concerned whether he could maintain his hiding place through another day. For what he was doing was absolutely illegal; he had no illusions on that score. And where before he had been nervous even bending the law, now he was flatly breaking it, and be damned to whomever found out. As long as he got the fisher first. That was his only reason for secrecy. He wanted no interference before he killed the animal.

It puzzled him now, how he ever could have felt tolerant toward the beast, when from practically the moment he had set his first trap, the fisher had been a thorn in his side. He wondered if there might not be some truth in what the old-timers said: that in the great, white silences, strange things happened to a man's thinking. Certainly his growing admiration of the fisher had died the moment he discovered the awful destruction the animal had wrought in that one trip up the trapline. He remembered the sick rage he had felt at the ragged mess the fisher had made of the superb pelts of fox, the martens, and the mink. In that one sweep along the line the fisher had cost him well over two hundred dollars.

It still seemed almost mystical the way the simple plan of how and where to trap the fisher had come to him. The idea, he thought, must have been born weeks or months ago, for suddenly, the plan was there in his mind, complete in every detail. He had cursed himself for not having thought of it much earlier.

He was good with his hands, but his lack of proper tools slowed him badly. It took him almost a day to cut an old, iron poker into three pieces, heat them, then hammer each into a tightly curved hook. Half the evening went in forming an eye on one of the shanks, then filing the hooks to a cruel sharpness. He stopped to eat, spent the next hour binding the shanks together with hard brass snare wire, then melted down the slugs of a dozen bullets and poured the lead over the bindings to seize them in place. The last hour was spent in fashioning and binding a little birch trefoil to keep the prongs apart. Finally, he snapped the chain of a number-five wolf trap to the shank and looked with approval on what he had made.

It was a small, but ruthlessly efficient three-prong

grapnel, a thing he had never used in trapping before, but something he was convinced would help him get the fisher in the sights of his rifle. The principle was very simple. Unlike a heavy clog, the grapnel allowed a trapped animal to run free. But the trail it left was unmistakable, and when the animal ducked into the underbrush, the hooks would snag and slow its pace to a walk. In the fisher's case the trapper knew he would head into the trees, and once the grapnel caught in the branches, it would spell the end. No matter how it tried, the animal could not hide from him thirty feet in the air.

He slept late, spent a few hours on the line, then returned to his cabin to rest. At first dark, he made his way around the lake, hiding his trail as much as possible in the heavy growth near the shore. He reconnoitered the clearing before creeping forward to set the trap. So cautious was he that it took him three-quarters of an hour to do the job to his satisfaction, but when he finally finished and dropped back behind the screen of scrub willows, there was not so much as a toeprint to show he had been near the place.

That first night was a failure. With the coming of false dawn, working swiftly, he dismantled the set and faded back to the trees, covering his prints with great care. Then he returned to his cabin, to sleep, to work a while, to eat, and in the first dark, to make his way around the lake and crouch among the willows until he felt it safe to reset the trap and grapnel.

Now, it was the waiting time again. He peered through the slender willow wands and up the clearing.

The moon was shining with a youthful innocence, spotlighting the declining drifts. He was pleased that even in a cross-light, he could see no sign of his work. He leaned his shoulders against a low boulder and shrugged to ease a fugitive itch. Idly, he thought of the pleasure of a steaming bath, now just a few weeks ahead of him. Just as idly, he thought of the past six months with its washbasins and harsh, yellow soap and speculated on just what strange quirk in his own character had made him take up this lonely life in the first place.

He let his mind wander for a few moments, then pulled it back to the present task, drew his rifle across his lap, and with the hunter's eternal patience, set himself to wait. Two hours went by before he saw much of anything, and then it was just a flicker of white moving palely through the shadows. His eyes were about to pass over it when he remembered the saddle of silvery fur draping the fisher's shoulders. Very tense and very alert now, the trapper sat forward and began a meticulous scrutiny of the shadows mantling the margin of the trees.

The fisher trotted down the northeast shore of the lake. Throughout the woods, wherever the snow had crusted thinly, were dark slashes of sodden ground and decayed, crumbling leaves and needles. The fisher wandered from one to the next, fascinated by the sight of sluggish, half-drowned earthworms that had struggled to the surface to escape the thaw waters flooding their underground galleries. Curiously, he tasted one, but spat it out immediately. He noticed that in the bare spots, though the earth was still laced with frost, there were the first signs of a moist sponginess.

Halfway down the shore, a faintly sickening smell drew him to the remains of a rabbit, killed earlier in the winter by an owl, but lost in a drift when the bird found it too heavy to hoist skyward. Now the frosty shroud was retreating, revealing the body. The fisher turned in disgust from the carcass, barely noticing the oval snowshoe print a few feet beyond. A momentary warning rang in his brain, but he refused to listen. Oval snowshoes belonged to the far shore of the lake. This was the friendly side.

The clearing around the old Ojibway's cabin was day-bright beneath the pockmarked moon. The fisher waited, listening, at the edge of the trees, as he always did. The steady trickling of water beneath the melting snow had stilled in the cool dark, for the earth needed the sun's warmth to wash away the last of winter. Only the few faint gurgles of water percolating through ant mounds and earthworm tunnels sounded in the quiet. He heard a bird fidget in the tree above him, awakened by the hoot of a distant owl. Faintly, from the direction of the old man's chicken run came the sleepy mutter of a hen. He thought he heard an animal rustle the willows near the lakeshore. There was nothing else. The world was at peace with the night.

As he pattered forward, the fisher peered toward the woodpile. In the little hollow at its peak, he saw the pale glimmer of an egg. Grunting happily, he broke into a trot, angling toward the slope at the rear as he had since the night when a frontal leap had collapsed the pile and crushed the egg. He touched a forepaw to the rearmost log and swung his hind foot forward to spring lightly up the ramped wood. His paw was already coming down when he caught the smell of the hidden steel. He stiffened, but his balance was gone, and his paw punched through the crisp snow crust to the trap beneath. He felt the roundness of the pan, and the sharp click of the trigger. He gasped as the toothed jaws bit into his upper leg. And then he screamed, a full-throated, bellowing screech of mingled pain and rage.

In the silence that followed, the rattle and clank of the grapnel and chain jangled with an unnatural shrillness. Near the shore, the willows rustled briefly as the trapper rose and pushed them aside to squint through the clear, blue moonlight.

The fisher's first leap took him halfway up the incline of the woodpile. He felt the trap come with him, jerking twice as the grapnel skittered over the bottom logs. He snarled and bit, but his teeth only rattled on the steel. He tugged, and the grapnel ripped clear. He stared at it, then sprang over and down the slope. Behind, the grapnel caught for a fraction of a second, bounced and slammed against the cabin with a solid, metallic thud. With the strength of the angry fisher driving them, the sharpened hooks slashed yard-long slivers from the wall before the grapnel ricocheted down, and with tremendous force, jammed into a gap between the ice-locked bottom logs of the woodpile and the foundation of the cabin. With a violent wrench the fisher hit the end of the chain and crashed to the snow. The force only served to bury the prongs deeper.

The trapper swore. He had planned on the fisher's escaping the vicinity of the cabin completely so he could hunt and kill it at leisure, without the old man suspecting it had been trapped on his property. A jammed grapnel was the last thing he had imagined.

He slipped the safety from his carbine and stood a moment considering. A shot would certainly wake the Indian, and a formal complaint charging him with trapping on private property would definitely cost him his license, if not for good, at least for a year or two. Simply leaving the animal trapped by the woodpile would be equally damning. With a nicety of logic, he realized he was left with just one alternative, to club the animal to death as quickly as possible and hope the old man was a sound sleeper. He clicked the catch back on to safety and gripped his rifle by the barrel.

The fisher could not really understand what was happening, how this thing that he had fought so successfully all winter had come to trap him here, in a place he had always equated with warmth and comfort and safety. He lurched to his feet and checked around him for further traps. Then he looked up and saw the squat, bulky shape of the trapper.

The fisher concentrated all his hate and pain into a single, ringing scream. It started low and ominously in his throat, then rose until it seemed to split the night. His entire world became the malevolent figure of the man, and he glared his fury toward it, the saddle of white fur a bristling silver ruff across his shoulders. Again he screamed, short and sharp and venomously. The trapper glanced toward the front of the cabin, then strode steadily on. The fisher threw himself against the chain, not conscious of the damage to his leg as the toothed trap cut a rowel down the belly of the muscle. For the moment, he was beyond pain, beyond fear, feeling nothing but an aching hunger to reach and rend the hulking shape before him.

The trapper stopped, frowning nervously at the enraged animal, calculating how best to go about his brutal business. The fisher tensed as he saw the man take a cautious step, shifting his grip on the rifle. He saw the stock begin to lift and set himself to lunge, waiting for the moment when the man moved within reach.

But the moment never came. Suddenly, sharply, the cabin door slammed. The trapper turned, the fisher whirled, as with a soft crunching of footsteps, the old Ojibway came around the corner. He was stripped to the waist, and the bluish moonlight washed all but the deepest hint of red from the thermal long-john bottoms he wore. He had only taken time to kick his feet into a pair of soft, ankle-high moccasins and grab a rifle before he left the cabin. Now, he levered a cartridge into the breech of his rifle.

Through the blood singing in his ears, the fisher dimly heard the Indian's soft, questioning voice and the guttural, harsh answer from the other. With a movement as smooth and liquid as one of his own, the old Ojibway slipped across the ground that separated them and knelt by the fisher's side. The old man began to speak, crooning the quiet syllables over and over, speaking the soft and coaxing words that gradually reached beneath the fisher's fury and soothed it. Imperceptibly at first, then with growing swiftness, the blindness drew away from the fisher's eyes and the controlled coldness crept in. A faint snarl still rumbled his throat, but he eased back on the trampled snow, and carefully arranging his throbbing leg, stretched out beside the old Indian, waiting for him to remove the trap. At that instant, the trapper lost control.

Even afterward, the man had no clear recollection of what he did, or why. He acted on blind impulse, born perhaps from the spiraling frustrations of the winter, but more than likely, simply from the sight of an old man kneeling beside an exceedingly dangerous animal and soothing it with words. His reaction was immediate—and violent. He threw his rifle to his shoulder and squeezed the trigger, but in his fury, did what he had not done since childhood. He forgot to release the safety catch. Frantically he thumbed it up and swung the sights to the fisher's head. He was too intent on the animal to see the old man swing his rifle single-handedly through a short arc at his hip.

The shots roared out almost simultaneously, the old man's possibly a tenth of a second ahead. But it was enough to throw the trapper's aim fractionally off. The fisher felt the stabbing burn as the bullet clipped the tip of his ear. The trapper started to go down, his body spun awkwardly about, his right leg kicked back at an ungainly angle. Then the bulky figure fell, and the fisher strained at the trap again.

The old Ojibway spoke to him quietly, rose catlike from where he crouched, and pumped another cartridge into his rifle. He strode across to where the trapper was struggling to push himself upright, and flipped the man's carbine away with the toe of his moccasin. Shaking his head, he knelt, put out his hand and slid the man's knife from its sheath. He reached toward the leg the man was gripping but the trapper cursed him and pushed his hands away. The old Ojibway spoke to him slowly and distinctly, as to a child, and with a singularly noncommital shrug, the trapper let his hands fall away. The old man split the seam of the trousers neatly and pulled the fabric back. There was a slow pulse of blood, black against the pallid skin, trickling down from a neat hole in the fleshy part of the calf. With an approving grunt, the Indian whipped off the trapper's belt, cinched it tightly around the man's thigh, and motioned him to hold the end. Then he returned to the fisher.

The animal looked deeply into the old man's eyes when the Indian knelt to force apart the trap's vicious jaws. He held the gaze while he carefully drew his leg free, then turned away to trace his tongue down the deep cuts. The old man watched while the fisher pulled himself to his feet, then sighed with relief when he saw the bone was unbroken. The fisher stood, testing his leg to see if it would bear weight. Then with a snarl, he crouched and began to limp toward the trapper in an ungainly, terrifying stalk. He saw the man go rigid and heard the Indian snap a single, imperative word. He looked back while pulses of anger ebbed and flowed through his aching muscles. The Indian spoke the single word again, emphasizing it with a slow shake of his head.

For the third time in his life the fisher felt contact with the old man. Though he could not think deeply enough to understand it, he now trusted the old man completely. It was as if, by accepting the closeness of the Indian *and* his rifle, he was somehow offering himself, momentarily, into the old man's keeping. And so he did as the Indian directed and broke off his attack. The trapper was still at his mercy, but he could not—must not—kill here and now.

With the killing urge gone, he was left with one desire, to return to his den. When he stopped beneath the downswept branches at the edge of the clearing, it was to see the Indian, with two rifles in one hand and the trapper's arm around his neck, helping the bearded man toward the cabin.

* * *

21

At midnight the clouds swept in above the lake and the rain came, cold at first, then warming as the overcast crowded closer to the earth. The drifts drank it in, sagged, and moldered swiftly away. Dawn brought light but no illumination, for all detail was smothered in the teeming rain, and the horizon of each creature's world shrank to a hundred bluish, hazy yards. The forest floor suddenly sprouted a squirming crop of earthworms fleeing their deep, flooded hibernaculae. Shrews raced shrieking from one to the next, stuffing themselves until they could barely move. Ants ran between the wiggling ranks, battling to save their own communities. A few succeeded, but most were lost as the shrews and birds, mice and voles made up for the hard winter by an orgy of stuffing.

The spring breakup began shortly after noon the next day. The first great thundercrash of the ice splitting up the lake snatched the fisher from a dreamless sleep. He slipped out of his den and cocked his ears about, searching for the cause. The grumbling died, then burst out again as the ice shattered diagonally from the old man's bay, across to the beaver's stream, and then back up to the north shore. The echoes caromed back and forth across the lake, subsiding slowly to a throaty, threatening growl. In their wake the woods lay locked in total silence, the animals and birds poised unmoving. The fisher too stood listening, waiting, until the hypnotic hush was broken by the scattered musket fire of smaller fractures across the four great pans of ice. Limping, he moved to the spit of the land, intrigued by the mystery behind the tumult.

The entire lake was writhing in long swells as the suddenly released pressure sent a turmoil of waves rolling across the surface. They pounded into the little bay, shattering the ice into hundreds of separate blocks. As the fisher watched, the chunks began to edge slowly into the clogged waters of the lake, forced by the steady pressure. In the marsh, the same process was taking place, but much more slowly, for many of the larger blocks were anchored by last year's tattered rushes and reeds. It would take time and the sun to destroy them, but already the fracture lines were cutting down the channels.

That night the fisher limped toward the trapline. Unbelievably, he found it gone. He covered the entire southern swing before the dawn, inspecting every set. The sets were still in place, the clogs lay in full view, even the bait sticks had been left behind. But not a trap remained. Only the pain of his bruised leg kept him from checking the northern leg of the line that night.

He was disturbed enough to awake early the next afternoon. The day was magnificent, but the fisher had no eyes for the fresh green catkins of the alders or the sensuous, yellow catkins of the willows and birches. His entire being was concentrated on the trapline, for it had been the thing of greatest importance for nearly half his young life, and its going gave a peculiarly empty feeling to the woods. By the time he reached the northern section, he was seriously perturbed, wire-taut beneath his careful, practiced questing.

The dull crack of steel on wood and the musical jingle of chain from somewhere close ahead sent him belly to the ground through the undergrowth. He was immensely relieved to discover it was the old Indian, kneeling in the damp to pry a stubborn staple from a clog. All afternoon the fisher became the Ojibway's shadow, following twenty yards behind while the man dismantled set after set, dropping the traps and snare mechanisms into his backpack. It became an exhilarating game when, mid-way through the tour, the old man began to suspect he was being followed. He tried every trick he knew to spot his watcher, but it was not until sunset that the fisher revealed himself. The old Indian took one look at the bright eyes and the sinuous form peering at him from a trail-side spruce and burst into laughter.

The fisher watched the Indian almost daily after that. He followed him down the western leg of the trapline and saw him dismantle each set. He tracked him to the trapper's cabin and spied from across the pond as he collected the bearded man's belongings and launched his canoe. As soon as the worst of the ice was gone, the old man loaded the bundles of peltries and paddled downstream, leaving the cabin door open behind him. The fisher padded toward the cabin and entered cautiously, sniffing distastefully at the smells of death—dead ashes, dead animals, and their meticulously treated dead-cold pelts; and the smell of the man, not dead, but slowly being smothered by the scent of evergreen.

And that was the last the western shore of the lake was to see of the trapper. The fisher wondered what had become of him, for though the ancient cabin by the pond was stripped and empty, his specter still walked the woods. But night by night, as the fisher moved along the old trapline, it was being driven home that the dangers were gone, the hidden jaws no longer lurked just out of sight. In one way he regretted their going, for he found hunting a considerably more difficult life than raiding. And yet, he found a warm satisfaction and a subtle sense of fulfillment in returning to the high-winging, pulse-pounding freedom of the chase. Gradually, with hunting taking more time and effort, he began to break away from his diurnal wintertime habits. He became once again a wanderer of the night and drowsed the spring-filled daylight hours away, at most coming out near sunset to lie a while upon his ledge. With the coming of twilight he returned to the nocturnal ways of his kind. Occasionally, when hunting was slim, he stayed out till dawn.

It was on such a morning that the fisher saw the trapper leave the lake for good. He had been ambling along the eastern shore of the lake, and the sun was half an hour up the sky by the time he approached the Ojibway's clearing. Not surprisingly, eggs were on his mind, so not till he was half out of the trees did the two figures at the water's edge attract his attention. He jerked to a stop and faded back under cover.

The trapper stood with a foot on the pier, the Ojibway slightly upshore. Neither was speaking; they were watching a dozen old-squaw ducks wheeling silently overhead. The birds craned their necks nervously toward the two men, below, whirling in interchanging patterns, until with sudden decision, they broke into a swift, attenuated spiral downward to the marsh. The men stood for a moment after they had gone, then the trapper bent toward the mooring of his heavily laden canoe. Before his fingers touched the rope, he straightened, turned, and in three quick strides, stood before the Indian. The trapper's arm went out, the old man met it, and they shook hands. The trapper swung around to his canoe, and limping slightly, boarded and pushed off from the shore. He did not look back, but stroked the bow lakeward and, to the sweet sound of the dipping paddle, swept northward through the spring sunshine.

The fisher followed along the shore, staying just within the compass of the trees, exactly matching his pace to the trapper's powerful strokes. He only was forced into a lope when the trapper cut across the end of the lake and ruddered easily around the shelving rock that anchored the stream that drained the lake. As the canoe felt the bite of the swifter waters, the fisher saw the man sit back to rest.

The animal was up and on the weathered shelf of granite that framed the streamhead before the canoe had covered fifty yards toward the first eastward jog of the stream. He sat back on his haunches, unconsciously posed to create an almost perfect picture, his sensitive but powerful head in profile, his coat gleaming, the saddle of silver fur a regal mantle across his shoulders. He was the only thing the trapper saw when he shipped his paddle and looked back to print the serene beauty of the lake on his memory.

Slowly, the fisher turned his head and their eyes met. Their eyes met and held and neither looked away. Neither moved. Neither made a sound. Neither reacted to the contact in any way, but each, beneath it, felt his emotions come alive. Oddly, the emotions were much alike, the man's and the animal's, though neither knew it. But each in his own way felt a sense of finality, as if in this time and at this place an end had been reached, or a beginning found of something that not the man, nor the animal could ever express. And then the moment was done.

The man moved first, but only because his canoe was nearing the bend. He was dwindling now in the fisher's eyes, but for a brief moment when the canoe passed two giant stream-side spruces, a beam of sunlight cutting down between the crowns caught and held it in a ring of morning light. That was the moment the trapper smiled and lifted his paddle to the fisher in a rather quizzical salute. Then the blade slashed down, cutting a creamy froth from the restless water, and the man was gone.

The fisher yawned. He blinked across his shoulder

at the sun and stretched mightily. He sighed and started the long trek down the northeastern shore toward his den. For a little while the image of the trapper persisted in his mind and then began to fade. The man was gone, and he was very sleepy, and all he really cared about was getting to his den.

But not really all. As he neared the old man's clearing his head came up, and he set himself to ponder how, on this most glorious of mornings, he might coax an egg from the old Ojibway. An egg—or two. That was a task worth setting himself.

EPILOGUE

THE MID-MAY SUN was magnificent, clean and ripe and indulgently warm where it spattered through the nodding branches to kiss the Indian's silver thatch. He was perched in the sentinel spruce, balancing easily on a lower bough that stretched out above the sheer point of the ridge a good fifteen feet. Sitting here overlooking the great green sea of spruce and pine he sought the pleasure the scene always gave him and found it curiously lacking. He could not conceive why.

Perversely, his thoughts kept drifting to the trapper. A surprising man, he mused, and a man with surprising depths. He had naturally expected an outburst after he had helped the trapper into his cabin and dressed his wound, but the man had been subdued, in a way almost chagrined. It had all come out the next day. The trapper was terribly ashamed at what he had done and acutely embarrassed that he had actually let an animal drive him to such lengths. The old Ojibway had held himself in as long as he could, but the trapper's crimson face and the earnest eyes above the beard had finally set him chuckling. The trapper had stared at him—first in surprise, then anger, then thoughtfulness—and suddenly had burst out with a whoop of laughter. It had been the start of one of the most pleasant weeks the old man had spent in a long time. Idly, he wondered whether the trapper would ever come back to the lake. Somehow he doubted it. No man likes to return to the scene of his defeats. In some ways, he thought, it's too bad.

Abruptly, he straightened. He understood his trouble now. It lay not in the day or the vista before him, but in himself. For the first time in many years, he was lonely for the company of men. The knowledge made him feel very old.

The sun was lowering toward the horizon. The old man cast his eyes up to where a goshawk swept his sunset circles against a sky deepening to a sadder blue. A breeze danced off the lake, bringing a touch of Maytime chill, and he shifted his weight to ease a rheumatic twinge. Older and older still, he grumbled to himself.

He jumped slightly at a sudden rattle of claws on bark, and again when the branch jarred beside him. But his face broke into a huge grin when he swung about to see the fisher stretch out on the limb at his side, the powerful head poised just above his hand. The animal glanced up at the copper face, then with a calculated insouciance, looked out across the evergreen sea. The old Ojibway chuckled, delighted anew by the fisher's way of moving like a silent wind. His eyes caressed the beautiful body. Despite his familiarity he was impressed. Nearly three feet from nose to tail, he mused. The fisher, he knew, would grow into the biggest he had ever seen. His glance drifted over the places where a nearly imperceptible difference in the lie of the fur told of injuries, at the hip, the flanks, and of course, the rather dapper saddle of silver across the deceptively slender shoulders. It's been a tough winter, the old man muttered, scarcely aware he was speaking aloud. Tough for both of us, and you just a year old.

The fisher lifted his eyes to the Indian's, and for a moment, the old man had the startling sensation that the animal understood exactly what he had said. He knew it was impossible, though the feeling surged to a height close to empathy when the fisher dropped his head, and with great respect and delicacy, touched the old man's hand with his nose and tongue. Impulsively, the man reached out and softly scratched the bullet-gouged ear. The fisher blinked, suffered the old man's touch, then circumspectly reached around, took the ball of the hand between his jaws, and gave it a firm but very careful nip. Together, he and the old Ojibway inspected the hand, the flesh indented, but the skin unbroken. Then, as one, both looked toward the lake where the reflections of the mounting clouds sailed softly across the sunset-stilled water.

As the sun touched the western rim, they turned and climbed slowly down. Side by side they walked along the ridge and together faded beneath the eternal trees. Here and there, the man stopped to scrutinize the signs of new growth, of starflower and adder's-tongue and the unfurling veined leaves of false Solomon's-seal. The fisher waited patiently at each pause, then walked beside the Indian to the mooring rocks and watched him slip into his canoe. The man tapped the gunwale near the bow, but the fisher only cocked his ears at the sound, then whirled and trotted away around the shore. The old man shrugged and pushed off smoothly across the shimmering water.

He docked the canoe and stood a moment on the shore, waiting for the fisher to swim the mouth of the stream. The animal flowed up on the land and shook himself dry in a sparkling, bluish mist of droplets. He padded swiftly forward, then stopped. The old Ojibway looked about and saw for the first time that the tenderly viridescent trees along the promontory across from his cabin were alive with warblers. Even in the languishing light, the tiny jewel-box birds seemed to flame with vivid contrasts of color. The old man had not seen such a rush of birds since the migrations of last fall. And once again he was aware of time, of its relentless passing, its finality, and of how casually he had spent its priceless gift through so many thoughtless seasons. The weight of his own mortality lay heavily upon him as he plodded to the cabin to fetch the patient fisher his egg.

The mood was still with him when he returned and knelt to watch the precision and grace with which the fisher cracked the delicate shell. The gurgling cry of a red-winged blackbird echoed cheerfully across the bay, trilling upward through the twilit hush. The old man glanced up in time to catch a figuration of dark wings rocketing up, then flashing down beyond the trees that hid the marsh. The sky still held a touch of daytime blue, but toward the zenith it was shading swiftly into indigo. To the north and south, the first few evening stars were beginning to glimmer, while in the west, very high and breathtakingly beautiful, stood three nocti-lucent clouds. They hung like flame-washed woodsmoke, so far above the earth that, though the sun was gone, they were still steeped in sunset radiance.

Carefully, as though he were afraid to shatter something very precious, the old man breathed a quiet sigh. The mood that had pressed so heavily on him all the afternoon was gone, for he had heard at last the message that for years the silent trees had whispered to him: age is of the body. Youth lies in the mind. And a man's a fool to think on time, when timelessness encloses him on every side.

There was an old Ojibway custom, seldom honored now, that when a man grew old, when the total of forgotten years outweighed the sum of years still left ahead, he would hunt a bear and kill it, and carve upon its shoulder blade a stroke for every year he wanted yet to live. Five years ago the old Ojibway had found such a bone, and smiling at his own foolishness, had cut five marks upon it. The same smile touched his eyes now as he entered the cabin and lit a fire against the spring evening's chill. Then he lifted a flat, roughly triangular shield of brittle, grayish bone from the mantle, and choosing his sharpest chisel, began to carve five more deep, meticulously straight grooves upon the weathered surface.

Outside, the fisher stretched himself sensuously and trotted toward the trees. Before he was beneath their shelter, his trot quickened to a graceful lope, for somewhere in the future just ahead, the porcupines were waiting. And he was still very hungry.